A SPANNER IN
THE CAR WORKS

A SPANNER IN
THE CAR WORKS

Memories of early years in the Car Industry

— DAVID CHAMBERS —

A CIP catalogue record for this book is available from the British Library.

ISBN 978-0-9571589-1-7

Book layout and cover design by Clare Brayshaw

Prepared and printed by:

York Publishing Services Ltd
64 Hallfield Road
Layerthorpe
York YO31 7ZQ

Tel: 01904 431213

Website: www.yps-publishing.co.uk

Contents

About the author

Born in Swansea in 1944, he with his parents moved to Bournemouth in the early 1950's. An interest in cars was fuelled by his brother in law who took him to racing circuits in Wales and then by his father who was persuaded to travel to Goodwood several times to see the TT races.

A fortunate education at Portchester School for Boys, where the basics of engineering were inculcated by like-minded teachers, ensured his development as a "petrolhead" and subsequent entry into the car industry where having started as an apprentice he eventually became an engineering director. He also lectured on metal forming at Warwick University. This life-long interest manifested itself with the purchase and running of classic cars and the development of possibly the largest non-commercial and extremely popular "Churchill Vintage & Classic Car Show" in the Cotswolds.

His other publication to date is "Tim China", a biography of a distant relative, and one the influential shapers of 19th century China. This led to several interviews on local and Welsh radio stations.

Foreword

The Pressed Steel Company in Oxford began as a joint venture in 1926 between William Morris and the Budd Corporation of America backed by American finance.

During this time it quoted for the manufacture of press tools and jigs and fixtures to a range of diverse companies. These are listed in App 1 and cover the period from 1926 to 1936. In the meantime, William Morris had seen the potential of unitary body construction as a lower cost route to making car bodies rather than the chassis based method of construction prevalent at the time. The other individual around this time who had this vision for producing cars in Europe was Andre Citroen whose "Traction Avant" led the way.

Pressed Steel continued to supply Morris Motors with bodies and body panels. Budd's finances deteriorated during the great depression forcing it to float and become a public company in 1936. Pressed Steel then started to supply bodies and panels from its press shop in "A" Building and subseqently from "R & S" Press and Assembly shops, as they were built, to the major car companies in the UK such as the Rootes Group, Rolls Royce and the Standard Motor Company. "A" Building ceased to be a press shop in 1962 going over primarily to body manufacture and supplying Morris's with bodies via the bridge across the by-pass. Rootes

Group Hillman Minx and Humber bodies went to the paint shop and then to the trim shop for delivery by Harding's Transport to Coventry.

The company rapidly expanded and built or acquired factories in Linwood, Swindon, Swansea and Llanelli and by 1968 was the largest independent car body and tool manufacturer in the world, supplying such well known companies as Volvo, Alfa Romeo and Hyundia . It branched out into aircraft manufacture by acquiring the Auster Aircraft Co. at Rearsby and had bought Oxford Airport at Kidlington. At the same time it was also the largest producer of railway rolling stock in the UK & manufacturer of the Prestcold refrigerators. All this required engineers to service the expanding empire.

The Preparation

"If you have a vision of a young man chewing gum, slouching around with his greased hair in Teddy Boy style incongruously sporting a bright red tie whilst the rest of his attire comprises a Gannex raincoat and drainpipe trousers, then that is a vision of a no hoper"
George Unwin

This crushing statement was announced one morning to my class at Porchester School in Bournemouth. It was delivered as a description of me by a pipe smoking, brown stained moustachioed geography teacher wearing a well worn tweed jacket that harboured a history of aromas accumulated and absorbed over a considerably long period of exposure to nicotine and beer with little, if any, consideration being given to the lightest sniff of the dry cleaners that were now starting to open up everywhere.

"Punch" Jarrett was the complete opposite, a small rotund man, slightly hunchbacked and possessing a rather beaky nose. Putting his arm over my shoulder he guided me to a notice board where he had just pinned up, a pink coloured article he had torn from the Financial Times. "This should interest you son" he said taking it down and placing it in my hands "You'll find it very interesting". It was an article about a new apprentice training school soon to be opened at Cowley near Oxford at a cost of a quarter of a million pounds. The company was not the Morris car works which most people had heard of – but the relatively unknown firm called "Pressed Steel."

Sometime before this in Cowley the tool drawing office had moved from the blue tiled exterior "main office block" which faced the by pass, to the new Engineering Block where the body engineers, jig & tool engineers and press tool engineers were grouped together. It was now due to expand again with the construction of a dedicated Tool Engineering Block and another three storey block for the training department, to include apprentice training, executive training etc.

In charge of the first move for the tooling department from the main office block was "Jock" Sutherland, a bushy eyed Scotsman blessed with a heavy accent and a short temper. If anything went wrong Jock would decide that it was Aubrey Timberlake's fault and he invariably gave him the mother of all dressings down in the middle of the office. When Jock was in fine form – purple faced with anger, fulminating and spitting voluminously he would vent his tirade on poor old "Timbers" who would stand there expressionless taking the full brunt of the verbal attack, the only visible sign of possible concern being a slight shuffling in his trouser pockets.

After he had finished his tirade, Jock would spin round and steam off for his office slamming the door and shaking all of the partition walling that enclosed it. "Timbers" appearance of being totally unaffected by the passing storm from Jock was born out when on one occasion, after rummaging around in his trouser pockets, he produced two large gooseberries. Placing them on the table he proudly asked the assembled audience "What do you think of them then?"

Whilst all of this was going on in Oxford, my favourite tutor "Punch" had decided to mentor me to prepare me for entering industry as I was just about the only pupil in his class who had expressed a genuine interest in engineering. I had bewailed the fact that the careers officer I had sat down with to talk over my aspirations of joining the car industry had shown total ignorance of any aspect of manufacturing and was trying to guide me into the hotel industry, due mainly to the fact that my father had been an hotelier throughout his life. Over the year I sat with "Punch" whilst he marked my work. He described his frustration at not being able to go into industry when he left school. He had looked wistfully at the heavy engineering companies that filled the area where he had been brought up, but had to settle for the only employment available at that time – *teaching* – and to get that he had to hitch lifts down to the south of England. This was the time of the 1930's depression. "Don't take notice of any advice from Civil Servants or government employees" He explained

"The roles of those in civil service jobs are so alienated from the real world of those who have to design and make. Be guided by what you want to do".

Now pupils have an uncanny way of finding out their teachers' weaknesses. "Punch's" was an allergy to oranges which the class soon latched on to. The very smell of the fruit would cause his eyes to run and for him to sneeze. To ensure this would happen on a regular basis, wedges of orange skin were placed under the four legs of his chair and copious amounts of juice squeezed into his waste paper bin each morning by my fellow pupils. Out of gratitude for what he had done for me I declined to take part.

The class did the same for "Bombshell" Renshaw taping stink bomb capsules to the feet of his chair. As he sat down they would be crushed and the stinking compound released.

"I would like to point out that the obnoxious effluvia has no effect on my olfactory organ" he declared, forcing us to examine our dictionaries to see if we had been successful or not. He also had the habit of coming into the classroom rattling off what we would be doing for the next hour whilst at the same time closing his eyes and leaning against the book cupboard. This he did instinctively until we repositioned the cupboard a few inches from its normal position causing him to lose balance. With careful tilting we had managed to get the contents firmly stacked and resting on the door. These now spilled out when he opened the door to the great delight of us pranksters.

Herbert Tinsley, a Lancashire man, gave me a very good grounding in the basics of engineering. He was the metalwork master at school and when I brought in a detail drawing of a Beam Engine from the "Model Engineer" magazine he suggested it would be an ideal project if we made a working model. I was willing to devote the next two years in his class doing it with him. All we had were the detail drawings. The project meant manufacturing a flywheel from strips of steel rolled and hammered into a circle and then finished off on a lathe, casting the cylinder in brass by making a sand mould, melting the brass and pouring it into the mould, machining the valves and beam from steel and making a boiler from riveted copper sheet. The project did not get off to a good start. The flywheel, to start with, had to be made from a steel strip heated in the furnace and then hammered over the pointed end of an anvil until it assumed the rough shape of a circle. "Tinners" decided that we would require more room for this operation.

"Grab the blunt end lad and we'll lift it off its stand".

With "Tinners" taking the pointed end and grunting in unison we started to lift the anvil. I could see he was in trouble. With me holding firmly on to my end of this cast iron lump I watched as the pointy bit slowly slid out of his greasy hands. There was nothing I could do as I watched the anvil descend onto his foot. "Jesus Christ" he bellowed then followed a staccato of "F's"……..as he hopped out of the workshop door into the quadrangle quartering it like some foul mouthed kangaroo. He disappeared for a while and then we heard him approach still swearing but this time sounding like a very slow diesel engine on tick over as by now the utterances had changed to "Bugger Bugger Bugger" finally heading for the nurses room for solace. He emerged the following day on crutches his foot encased in a plaster soon to be decorated on the heel by the very swear word he had repeatedly used applied by an adventurous pupil crawling under his desk with a crayon.

The next calamity for "Tinners" was not that far away, we had to cast the brass cylinder. I made a wooden pattern of the cylinder in the woodwork class and gave it to him. He then placed it in a casting box and packed sand around it. This was then removed so that its impression was left in the sand. This procedure was done in two halves so that when the box was put together the brass could be melted in a crucible in the furnace and then poured into the cavity left by the pattern. To hold itself in shape the sand had to be slightly damp and as this was our first attempt we had no idea of the degree of moisture that was required. The molten brass was poured into the mould by "Tinners". As he did this there was a high pitched hissing and spitting sound followed by a pretty loud explosion. The sand had been too damp and the trapped steam exploded like a grenade, shattering the mould and spraying molten brass everywhere. "Tinners" looked up from a scene of total destruction, each lens of his glasses displayed an ink blot shape of solidified brass, his overalls smoking from a hundred craters created by the smaller splatters.

"It's a good job I wasn't wearing my best specs" he said.

"Now lads, you won't let the headmaster know of this will you".

After much testing we got the mixture right and successfully cast the cylinder and other items. The forged flywheel ring had spokes which were joined to the hub and was then mounted on a lathe and turned true.

This was my second explosive event in the metalwork class. Some months earlier we had a boy placed in the school from a Borstal institution – ostensibly to rehabilitate him into some semblance of normal life. He was a large lad and took great delight in beating up anyone who got in his way. It was not long before he had broken into the local Territorial Army Depot and arrived one morning with several rounds of munitions – larger than bullets more like small shells. He gave one to me and being of an inquisitive nature I suggested that we cut it in half, nothing interesting appeared to emerge from it so we chucked into the workshop furnace when "Tinners" was out and took shelter around the workshop,- nothing happened even though it was glowing red hot. After it had cooled down I decided to put it in a vice and using a centre punch hit the copper detonator cap with one sharp blow from a hammer. I can still in my mind's eye see the cap coming off as if in slow motion followed by a tremendous explosion and black smoke. "Tinners" , having returned, almost fell off his chair shouting out "Who the hell did that?" It was pretty obvious really as I had a ring of silent classmates around me staring with their mouths wide open, the real giveaway was a black stained leather apron I was wearing with curly wisps of smoke emanating sporadically.

I was immediately sent to the head's study for an inquisition. Fortunately "Borstal Boy" was a bit of a coward and walked behind me begging me not to snitch on him and asking what he should do. Quickly, I told him to throw whatever he had left over the school's rear wall. During my interrogation by the Headmaster I was told that unless I had a valid explanation I would be expelled. Delaying the proceedings for as long as I could to allow for the disposal of the ammunition. I told the Head I had found it in the road that morning and praying that my instructions had been followed I took a delegation of teachers through the school's back entrance along the wall and with my heart in my mouth came across four shiny shells on the pavement. The punishment was one hour's detention every night for a month but importantly I avoided a beating up and the bonus was – "Borstal Boy" protected my interests for the rest of the time he was at school which only lasted for about six months until his ultimate act of trying to strangle the geography teacher led to his extraction from school.

It was during this period that I really got interested in the car industry.

When I was about eleven I saw what I regarded as the most stylish of cars parked by Bournemouth Pier. I asked Dad what it was and was told that it was a 1938 Triumph Dolomite.

Meanwhile, in Cowley the Tool Engineering department was now consolidating, having started off with Joe Ball in charge and Freddie Griffiths, Reg Marriot and Jimmy James under him. Jimmy was the rising star and was put on to the executive development plan which led to him being sponsored to attend Yale University. On his return he appeared in stylish suits but always with trouser legs about three inches shorter than they should be. Phil Haines was put in charge of the Die Planning department which spurred Reg Marriot to analyse what he had to do enhance his own career prospects hitting upon the idea of exuding the air that he was "Managerial Material" He adopted the persona of a country gentleman, coming to work dressed in a tweed jacket and tweed cap. To reinforce this he would go to Banbury cattle market to mix with other country types. This eventually came to a sudden and expensive conclusion when suffering from a heavy cold which resulted in much nose blowing and a flurry of aggressive wiping with a large red handkerchief he found he was the proud owner of a calf.

It wasn't long before I was buying car magazines and when Dad got me an NSU scooter I was off to Goodwood to watch the TT and Formula 1 races with Stirling Moss, Roy Salvadori, Innes Ireland and a young Jim Clark battling it out in a Cortina with Sir Gawain Bailey in a Ford Galaxy, a monster of a car. Clark overtaking on the corners as Bailey wallowed around them and then the sheer brute force of litres of V8 power allowed Bailey to forge past Clark again. Heady stuff for a budding petrol head when driving skills really counted. My battle was driving back on a 75cc scooter with the throttle permanently fully open in order to make any headway with the grossly underpowered machine. Arriving back home from this three hour endurance trip, I parked the bike in the garage; the engine glowing in the dark. After turning off the ignition it would still chunter on until it stopped of its own accord. Like a zombie, I would head back into the house barely noticing my pet dog, Bryn, a Welsh Cardigan Corgi. I would sit down whilst my Mum got me a drink. I was still mentally on that scooter with the sound of the engine buzzing in my head. After a while normality crept in and I returned to the land of the living. But cars were the opium of this individual.

"Johnny" Marsham my final form head teacher was a bear of a man. Your first introduction to him at school was to stand in a group whilst he berated you, shouting how he hated kids and displaying surprising agility as he pranced about waving his cane, thrusting and parrying like a demented fencer. From that time on you lived in fear of his presence. He would enter a noisy playground sneering at everyone and a hush would descend until everyone was sure he had gone. If he entered a classroom you would quake with fear for if he felt that any teacher had been soft on any punishment he would make up for it in no uncertain terms with his cane. He was the Mr. Nasty to the Headmaster's Mr. Nice although the head was a strong disciplinarian and was driven to make the school equal to any Grammar School, a feat he ultimately managed to achieve in both academic and sporting disciplines and being rewarded with an O.B.E.

The final 6th form at school was "Johnny's" class. Imagine the pent up fear that we all felt as we sat at our desks waiting for the bomb to hit us. In he tramped sneering and leering over the class as he clocked every boy's face. "Finch" he roared, "You must think your pretty good mustn't you, no detentions, no canes, a general spineless goody goody. I'll be watching your every move boy". Turning suddenly he said "This chap" and putting his hand on my head "Has been nothing but trouble from the day he arrived, he's got the sort of character that I like." As my chest puffed up with pride and a smile spread across my face the hand that had been gently patting the top of my head suddenly gave me a sharp cuff on the ear. "But I'll be watching you too and that I trust will be the last time I have to hit you". From then on he would defend his class pupils to the hilt for any misdemeanour that was carried out but God help you on returning to the classroom.

The first thing that Johnny found out during his "assessment" of our capabilities was that we were about nine months behind schedule in mathematics. This was due mainly to the regular maths master being taken ill with TB thus causing mass disruption since we all had to be tested for the disease and the young inexperienced supply teachers really were easy meat for us. [Such as putting a smouldering rag in a desk or as he sat, quietly, filling up the turnups of his trousers with water]. Johnny in his usual brutal fashion did a crammer, compressing months of teaching into a few weeks. Instead of shouting and bawling, this time he took us quietly through the history of maths. How the Arabs developed the numerals, why the Roman numerals were useless for calculations, he taught us the shortcuts you needed to save time in exams All of a sudden mathematics became an interesting subject and we soon we ran out of books in the school library and more had to be sent to feed the renewed interest. That year we had the highest GCE pass rate in the school's history and it was all down to that remarkable man who was held in the utmost respect by all of his pupils.

Come GCE time nine subjects were taken and I failed in only one –English Literature. The subjects were Shakespeare's Twelfth Night and H.G. Well's The First Men in the Moon. The latter was naturally interesting and I'd memorised the Shakespeare play from start to finish but still failed. Having had the results meant that the pressure was now released and it was time to enjoy the new found freedom. The last day at school was full of practical jokes. A toilet pan had been rescued from the scrap heap of the local builders' merchant and cemented to the roof of the canteen only to be taken down very quickly by the Fire Brigade as the roof, having been constructed of asbestos, was considered unsafe to climb on! Mr Harrison, a flash individual, had a two toned green 11/2 litre Jaguar. In those days of relative honesty it was always unlocked. With a helpful gang it did not take long to push the car round a couple of blocks to our sister school Avonbourne. On positioning the vehicle in the middle of the girl's school playground, poor old Finch was set upon, stripped of all clothing and left inside for the delectation of the girls to view when they came out for their break. Job done the gang returned for the final assembly and farewell speech from the headmaster. Instead it was Johnny Marsham who got onto the stage and with his sneering look, scanned the mass of pupils before him declaring that Mr. Harrison's car had gone missing but he knew who the main culprit was as he was wearing a somewhat brightly coloured gaudy outfit. In a sea of blue blazers I stood out like a beacon – the only one wearing a bright canary yellow pullover. He went on to say that he would give those involved thirty minutes to return the car before he called the police. He slowly turned his face towards my direction with just the slightest hint of a smile. Crouching down I made a hasty exit weaving in and out of the assembled masses, gathering up fellow conspirators en route running hell for leather to the girl's school where the shrill squeals of feminine delight could be heard well before we could reached the Jag through the throng of excited females, inside the car was a cowering Finch desperately trying to cover up his bits and pieces.

So ended what had been a most enjoyable period of education, now all that remained was to wait for the GCE results and earn some much needed cash working as a temporary in a large Bournemouth hotel. Hopefully I was to progress from earning £11 an hour in a hotel kitchen by becoming an engineering apprentice in the car industry.

In Swindon, at this time, a new boss was put in charge of the Tool Drawing Office – Des Allsopp. The original manager, Spen Copestake had been replaced by Dave Blissett and shortly after that Des had brought his old pal, Bill Durman, from Cowley to work with him as the office grew rapidly in size. Other recruits being brought in from local industries were Barry Wheeler and Gary Kirk who became the foundation in the Press Tool Design Office building up its expertise at Swindon.

Swindon expanded rapidly producing pressings for the UK & continental car industry. Eventually "C" building was constructed and at the time it was the largest press shop in Europe. Added to this was car body assembly.

The Induction

You must be mad, in fact your potty!
                                              "Arthur" Fallowfield

"Arthur's" outburst echoed around the apprentice training school, the words spilling out from a mouth contorted with pent up venom caused by the frustration of being on the receiving end of a sustained period of taunting from me. No sooner had he uttered the dreaded phrase, when he realised that a eureka moment had just occurred and with a look of supreme satisfaction, he gleefully managed to turn the tables – "Your Potty – Potty Chambers!" a moniker I had successfully avoided since living in England. Up until then I had promoted my Welsh background so that I was always known as Taffy, "Arthur" Fallowfield, so called because of the character in the radio show "Round the Horne featuring Kenneth Horne and Kenneth Williams. My nickname has now been with me for the rest of my life so much so that many years later, whilst visiting a toolmaker in Germany, I was greeted with the usual handshake and

"Ah Potty Chambers". It happened again in China where several of my workmates had located themselves and thought it was great fun to tell the Chinese that it was very respectful to call me by my "Honourable Title".

Before all of this, on my first visit to Oxford and for my potential job interview I carried my beloved beam engine to display to the induction panel at Pressed Steel to prove that I was worthy of being recruited for a position in their new training school. Naivety had prevented me from knowing that the company at that time invariably only took on local apprentices or those who had members of their family working in the factory. The beam engine did the trick – I was to be the first apprentice taken on from outside these normal parameters – "Thank you Herbert Tinsley and the pain you went through". Arriving at Oxford the day before my first interview I had been booked in to stay at the Crown Inn in Cornmarket. It was a very old structure with floors so grossly undulating that they defied you to maintain your balance as you walked around the rooms. The landlord was a friend of my father and had told him that I would be well looked after. After a hearty breakfast and having asked how far the factory was from Carfax I worked out that I could easily walk it in the time and save the bus fare. It was a warm summer morning and having strolled up the High Street and found the Cowley Road I started to get a little concerned when it appeared that it was taking a little bit longer than I had been led to believe. The beam engine was now starting to weigh heavy. Somewhere near the bus depot I decided to ask a passer-by how long it would take to get to Pressed Steel. It was a good twenty minutes away, I had only given myself thirty minutes for whole trip. Luckily for me at school I had got my "colours" for cross country running and broke into a trot arriving at the factory gate hot, flustered and in a bit of a panic.

Cyril Bennett [head of apprentice training] luckily, was running slightly behind schedule, so lateness was not an issue. Having been ushered into a small room with two girls typing furiously I sat down and waited my turn for the interview. What with the physical exertion and nervous anticipation I was already pretty hot from the run up the Cowley Road and yet I was not cooling down but getting hotter and hotter. One of the girls seeing my predicament suggested I moved to the next seat as that would release my trouser leg from the steaming kettle spout and they could also get on with making some tea.

The interview went quite smoothly. Cyril sat in his chair with his hands forming a triangular arch in front of him, looking very ecclesiastical as if he was about to dispense some divine judgement. At his side sat his personal secretary, dressed entirely in black like a Victorian aunt, taking occasional notes and adding further to the ecclesiastical ambiance of the proceedings. Later on I was to learn that Cyril's secretary had been with him a long time and after working with him for some years she became his wife. Somehow their appearance certainly belied that they could have had a relationship at work.

I was very lucky in the answers I gave. To help pass the time before the interview I was given some cards to fill in. On one card were several columns of words and you were invited to ring three of these words that would best describe your character, Ambitious, Thoughtful and Bashful were those that I chose. In my ignorance – not having come across the word bashful before or have any knowledge of its true meaning, I thought it meant full of bash – being aggressive – and thinking that that they would be looking for someone who had a forceful character, I highlighted it. On my being called in for the interview, Cyril was sat going through the cards looking at the various adjectives ringed. "Do you know you are first interviewee I've had who has honestly admitted to being of a retiring nature. How do manage to overcome it?" Thinking quickly I said "I force myself to do things even if it is out of my comfort zone." Cyril was duly impressed with this answer and made sure it was written down. "Now where do you see your career going in the Pressed Steel Company?" Sitting there I replied that it would be a bit presumptuous of me to plan a career path on my limited knowledge. All I wanted to do at this stage was to be in car body design and to progress as far as I could in as short a time as possible. This brought about further grunts of approval and further note scribbling. At the end of the session I was told that I would receive notification of the success or otherwise of my interview within two weeks and this would tell me if I was to be inducted as a student apprentice. The caveat to it all was that if my GCE results were not up to the standard expected then I could be offered a craft apprenticeship. A further hurdle to this was that Pressed Steel still had their own set of entrance exams which I still had to pass to see to which engineering discipline I was most suited to.

Back I came again to Pressed Steel to sit in a building called The Poplars which sat incongruously in the middle of the factory site. Originally it had been a poor law school and was incorporated into the factory infrastructure as it expanded, as were its gardens and walnut trees. It was here that the 1961's potential intake of apprentices, at my session there must have been about forty, sat down and completed what I learnt later in my career were psychometric tests designed to evaluate your prowess at solving mechanical and design problems and were also meant to see how you fitted in with teamwork. A day of that and I was only too ready to catch the train home to Bournemouth. This relaxed sojourn did not last long. First I got my GCE results. I had passed everything except English Literature. How could that be? I had memorised Twelfth Night from start to finish and always got top marks in the tests. Never mind - I WAS IN THE CAR INDUSTRY, and furthermore I was to be in the Body Design Office – GREAT! The next step was to make arrangements to move to Cowley. The firm had found me "Digs" at a Mrs. Bakers in Rymers Lane for 10/6 a week. I was to earn £4.17.6 a week but out of that would come rental for overalls and payment for safety shoes, leaving me with sweet Fanny Adams to live on let alone get back to my girlfriend each weekend *and I'd given up the opportunity of earning £11 a week* as a general factotum in an hotel kitchen!! It was to be another two years before I reached anything near that sort of income.

I duly caught the train to Oxford to start my new career, waving my girlfriend goodbye at Christchurch station. Her Mum had cut me some doorstep sandwiches to make sure I would survive the rail journey. This was marvellous, I could make them last one maybe two days – after all they were no worse after two days in a plastic bag than the British Rail offerings one could see at each station. Safely ensconced in Cowley I had to work out a system to survive on my limited income. I soon found out that the pubs had games of darts in winter and Aunt Sally in summer. Choosing the right pub you could sit down with half a cider for the night. The teams were often very generous and any surplus sandwiches or pickled onions were soon passed round for others to share especially the sad looking individual with his half of cider. This helped supplement my landlady's offerings of various

Sainsbury's pies or sausages, all of which were accompanied with a portion of chips and baked beans. My sister also sent me food parcels to start with. Winter time was particularly grim. The Digs were so cold that I would put more clothes on to go to bed than I wore to go to work! Again, my sister came to my salvation when she gave me a pullover she had knitted for her husband Fred. This heavy woollen apparel which had started out as a normal large size chunky pullover had, with each wash, grown a bit larger. When I received it, it was down to my ankles but I could roll it up and double it to provide maximum insulation to go to work at seven in the morning. During the winter of '62 it was rarely possible to wash at my digs as the pipes hadn't thawed at six in the morning so I had to do this in the toilets at work. Mrs. Baker had been thoughtful and filled the basin with water the night before but by the morning it too had frozen solid. Keeping warm at night required some more lateral thinking and this was achieved by enrolling for four night classes at Headington Technical College [Now Brookes University] as part of my HNC course. Any spare evenings were spent in Temple Cowley library where a lovely husband and wife team administered the logistics of storing and remembering which books certain customers would like. They were so knowledgeable that any query was nearly always answered within minutes and when I went in they would pass me books that they were sure I would be interested in that they had obtained from other libraries. I became quite knowledgeable on Inca and Aztec history but at least it meant I was in a warm environment.

It was around this time that Pressed Steel, having built a new factory at Swindon with the largest Press Shop in

Europe, started to recruit tool designers there. Some of these lucky individuals were later to become firm friends. The toolroom at Cowley was also one of the largest in Europe.

On the way to Pressed Steel from my "digs" I had to walk along the Garsington Road past "The Morris" works. Old Cowley itself was a small area of run down cottages, some of them thatched, that had been left to rot away, an opportunity lost due to a lack of imagination that could have created a delightful relaxed area. Instead I watched it all being torn down and a typical soulless sixties concrete monolith built in its place where the cold winds would blow and people scurried, unsmiling, dodging the rubbish that seemed to spiral in the cyclone created by the large open square fed by the impersonal alleyways arriving from its extremities. For some reason they decided to keep the "Nelson" pub. Maybe someone thought that a brick built 1930's building stuck incongruously in the middle of all this would lend some character to the surroundings. It would take another forty odd years to pass before the penny dropped and it was pulled down. The walk from my digs in Rymers Lane passed all this and what really fascinated me as I went past Morris Motors every morning was to peer through metal fence to see the vehicles being prepped for sale. I could not believe my eyes that as Morris 1000 vans were being finished off to the Post Office specification, in between these there were green Post Office Telephone vans being finalised. These were still being built to a fifty year old design based on the E Series platform. Some Civil Servant – to Lord Nuffield's delight- must have placed a massive order in the late forties forgetting that vehicle design does evolve and improve year on year.

During 1962 the gaps in the fence started to be blocked off with wooden planks and you knew something was up – a new car was being produced! As I walked in the early morning darkness the shape of a very modern looking car would pass by, it was the ADO 16 or Morris 1100. Later early morning glimpses would show the Riley, Wolseley and MG versions out on test. On the other side of the road there was a long brick building with a large clock over the door. Inside were the director's offices – wood panelled and very imposing. I never thought that one day I would be ensconced in one of them when I was made to leave the body plant, as it had then become known, by Andy Barr, Manufacturing Director of Austin Rover and go over to the assembly plant as Quality Manager.

I particularly remember one New Year's Eve as having spent Xmas at home – it must have been 1964 – I boarded the train for Oxford in blizzard conditions. All appeared to go well as journey progressed, the trains were slightly late, changing at Basingstoke and then Reading the final stage to Oxford was starting to go quite slow. The first sign of trouble was when the lights kept flashing on and off. The speed of the train gradually reduced to crawl and we finally came to a halt stuck in snowdrift somewhere in Oxfordshire. It was cold and dark. A ticket inspector came along and informed us that they would be reversing and attempting to charge through the drifting snow. After about an hour of shuffling to & fro the train made slow progress to Oxford station. It was now early morning so I decided to make my way to the works on foot as I knew that No. 4 gate would be open and heated. Trudging knee deep in snow I got to the Garsington Road roundabout and believe it or not, a taxi was charging down the By-Pass swaying from side to side barely under control. It appeared to be heading straight for me so I dropped my suitcase and legged it, the taxi just missing me. Looking back I saw my suitcase had burst open so I now had clean soggy clothes as well! What was more galling was that if I had stood still the taxi would have spun around me. A cold, soggy, shivering individual finally made it to the security box at No. 4 gate. I was ushered in and made to sit down, given a cup of tea, sat down in front of a two bar electric fire, my wet clothes were hung on the back of a chair to dry off. What a way to celebrate New Year's Day! Next morning I was the first to clock in and regaled everyone who cared to listen about my adventurous journey.

The first days at the apprentice training school meant making new friends. There were at least a hundred craft and student apprentices in the system with a fresh intake being taken on each year and we were then sub divided into groups of ten or twelve. We had about six to eight weeks in each class where we learnt the fundamentals of our craft plus the art of trying to get each other into trouble. Each session concentrated on one element in the design and manufacture of car bodies and their tooling. They comprised Pattern Making, Welding, the Machine Shop where you learnt to operate the different types of machines used in tool manufacture, Metal forming and finally Body Design & Tool Design. Before you were let loose in the factory Sam Brogden, the safety officer, came in to give you a lecture. His opening gambit was to point at someone and shout "catch" throwing a round object at you which turned out to be a glass eye. There then followed a lecture on wearing safety glasses. Then he said never do what he had just done under any circumstance, that is to throw objects assuming they would be caught. Not so long ago previously some poor individual had tried to head what he thought was a rubber ball but was in fact a steel one and ended up brain damaged. After an hour of being told the danger of having long hair, loose clothing and wearing rings accompanied by photographs of individuals who had been scalped and a particularly gruesome one of a finger with the tendon streaming from it, you left wondering if you had entered the right profession. After going through this indoctrination you were let out into the factory to practice the tools of your trade.

From the induction tests I had taken earlier on, it had been confirmed that my desire to enter the Body Design office had been ratified and we were split into groups to go through a twelve-month training programme in the newly built training-school to make us ready for our chosen career. Each week started with a change of overalls where we all gathered to hand in our dirty apparel and pick up a fresh-set. This gradually morphed into more of a social occasion where you swapped stories and found out what was happening in the other courses. These changes were imperative as overalls invariably got oily from the machines we were working on or, more likely, from the randomly launched balls of grease that were aimed at you by your fellow inmates when you least suspected it. The most impressive demonstration of grease balling was carried out by Pete Henry who would wait for the supervisor, Albert Song, to leave the workshop and then he would take a blob of grease out of a drum and passing it from the finger of one hand to the other, carefully fashioned a perfect grease ball moving it gradually to the end of his forefinger ready for launching. He improved on this managing to increase the range and velocity by using one of the steel rules from his toolbox bent spring like with the grease blob on one end. His best effort was when he flicked his missile at an acute angle slightly behind "Ticky" Bowerman This blob went at an exceedingly high velocity and managed to enter the gap between "Ticky's" forehead and his safety glasses. The sudden loss of vision caused by the greaseball careering across both lenses caught Ticky by surprise, who, for a moment thought that he had lost his vision. His second mistake was to turn around with his mouth open in protest just in time for the next glob to find its way into his mouth. All hell then broke loose with grease flying across the workshop in every direct splattering as they impacted on the walls and ceiling in a slimy brown trail. Albert returned to a serene scene of a group of diligent apprentices working on their machines. In the background the white and cream workshop had been transformed into a mucky grease stained brown colour. For the rest of the week we were made to clean off everything with white spirits. From then on only occasionally did a random greaseball find an unsuspecting target.

The smelly grease stained overalls were returned to the storeman "Sid" who issued the clean ware and dispatched the dirty to the laundry contractors. As we got to know Sid better he let on that he used to be a signwriter at the local brewery and most of the local signs were his handywork. Rather foolishly he let, that he did nip out and "do" the odd "commission" during the week, proudly stating that he had been asked to paint a sign above a new boutique shop to be opened in the Cowley Road whilst the owners were away on holiday in Scotland. The sign looked very impressive and Sid was justifiably pleased with the end result. It read "Serendipity" in a fine flourishing flowing scroll – Gold on Green. Sid was clearly talented. That day I phoned him on the internal works phone and impersonating an irate shop owner blasted him off for cocking up the sign.

"Look here, I'm on my way to pick up my wife in Scotland before she comes down to her shop and I thought I would have a quick look to see how your work was progressing, what the hell do you think you are doing you've miss spelt the shop name!"

"I haven't", spluttered a confused Sid," I've done it just as she asked me to, I took down the spelling letter by letter from your wife?"

"Look, I'm putting the money up for this venture, I've printed off all the business paperwork and believe me it's called Serenadipity after my wife's name - Serena not Serendipity which every other blasted shop of this type is called!"

"I'll go down straight away Sir" said Sid "and correct it and she will not know there was an error"

Off went Sid and redid the sign. A day later poor Sid got another blasting off from the owner over his incompetence. We next saw him in the tool store at work complaining about some toffee nosed fart who couldn't organise the proverbial in a brewery.

Back at the training school we were working our way around the skills course. In the welding area under the tutelage of "Noddy" Eacot we went through the different methods of welding which were then put into practice when we sat in enclosed booths either doing gas or arc welding. When a trainee was engrossed in the difficult art of welding within these booths he was oblivious to what was going on around him which could manifest itself by actions taken by a fellow apprentice such as the weaving of wire through the laces of his safety boot and then the tack welding of the wire to the booth where he sat. The same principle was employed on the belt buckles on the overalls with the wire threaded through the buckles on overalls and then tacked to the booth. The results were hilarious when the unsuspecting victim got up to go away with the sound of ripping overalls or swear words as they lost balance The most spectacular act we saw involved Pete "Hairy" Henry, who was particularly good at gas welding, so good that Noddy asked him to show the rest of us how it should be done. With a group of us stood around him and Noddy beaming over his shoulder with pride at "Hairy's" prowess he started doing a perfect seam weld accompanied by several mutterings of approval from us observers. The weld was smooth and even as the maestro controlled the gas torch and puddled the welding wire at just the right speed along the two pieces of metal to be joined leaving a perfectly smooth joint behind the flame and wire. Carried away by his own success, and with a bit too much confidence for some reason, he managed to stop moving his left hand, which was holding the wire, and slowly carried on with blow torch up and across his wrist seemingly unaware that his skin was blistering up like the top of a rice pudding. This was a slightly more serious injury –the welding school was getting a bad reputation! He was packed off to the works hospital where the nurse made him drop his trousers and have a tetanus injection in the thigh – a normal occurrence as she was well known to the younger attendees when after a long gaze she would say,

"Just a little prick!" before administrating the preventative mixture.

The next session was in the machine shop. When the training school was built by Kingerlee's it was reputed, at that time, to have the largest unsupported pre-stressed concrete floor in the UK. Unfortunately, the architects were unaware, or did not appreciate that machines were to be installed in an area that they had clearly marked "Machine Shop" and when the said pieces of equipment were delivered the structural engineers would not allow some of the weightier units to be bolted to the floor for fear of upsetting the integrity of the building. It did not take long for this loophole to be exploited and Ernie Horne was the first victim. A meticulous chap by nature, primed by a morning lesson on how to operate the horizontal mill – he made sure that all the settings were correct to machine a block of steel. One part of the lesson should have been *If you leave your machine for the smallest amount of time recheck the settings on your return.* Mysteriously, someone had altered them all, one maximising the depth of cut, one slowing the rotation speed of the cutter and another, the speed of the feed. Ernie came back and pulled down the handle to start the operation. There was a rather loud clunk as the cutter took a mall bite out of the steel on its slow rotation. The next sound was a loud crash as the cutter tried to take an oversized chunk of metal out of the block being machined. Ernie leapt into the air at about the same height as the machine. The next crash harmonised with the sound of a cutter disintegrating, Albert Song the supervisor rushed out of his office legs furiously rotating like some cartoon character as he attempted to get to the machine before it took another large lurch towards oblivion. Ernie was now in a state of shock and was rooted to the ground as he imagined the machine would self-destruct. No one owned up to resetting the machine, so he was blamed for not setting it correctly.

The next victim was Dave Jarrett. He was on the capstan lathe. When operating this machine as well as concentrating on your turning project you had to make constant checks of the pockets in your overalls to ensure that some kind soul had not placed the coolant hose there and turned on the pump. The natural waterproofness of the overall gave the instigator just enough time to make an exit before the innocent trainee felt the awful wet sensation of gallons of coolant flowing down his trouser leg.

The fitting course was run by Don Harris. It transpired that he was the uncle of my mate Paul "Arry" Goddard and we accused him of fast-tracking Paul's career progress. Under Harris's tutelage we made set squares and other tools plus a miniature flat table made from a square of cold rolled steel [CRS]. This was achieved by smearing it in engineers blue and sliding it over a calibrated flat surface table. This would leave clear areas where the high spots were and the residual blue stain indicating the lowest. Then using a very hard scraper tool to remove a few "thou" from these high areas repeating the process until about 95% of the surface showing blue and therefore flat. By dexterous use of the scraper you could obtain lovely artistic patterns on the surface something you now only see in old engineering museums.

Several years later when I was made a Director at the Swindon plant Don sidled up to me and said rather sarcastically

"I hope you are capable of taking the pressure that goes with your new position, I wouldn't put money on it".

Next, we went to the metal forming class run by Roger "Ty" Harding. Roger would always preface any statement with "In actual fact" and if he was feeling particularly loquacious he used "Actually in actual fact". Here we made a toolbox with a "Gullwing" lid to access the removable tray that was fitted inside –all from scrap sheet steel brought up from the factory. I still have that box and the funnels made in the class – the funnels comprised a standard round conical one, a rectangular one topped one and the one that was most difficult to make, a swan necked design for pouring liquid into difficult to access containers. Besides making these from bits of flat metal we had to draw templates so that each component part of the funnel could be cut from the metal sheet and then gradually formed into the 3D finished product.

Back in the machinery class "Flossie" Coppock was leaning nonchalantly against the wheel of the horizontal grinder having a chat, a foolish act at the best of times. All of a sudden a loud "Yeeeeyow" echoed around the machine shop and Flossie, who was not the fastest mover, leapt away from the machine as the grinding wheel sped away at high revs. The reason for his alacrity became clear when the grinding wheel displayed some coloured rings – just like Saturn- green where Flossies overall had been, red where his pullover had been and the thinnest of blue lines for his shirt. His quick reaction meant that only the slightest graze was inflicted so not a trace of blood was evident, however, the next training department – pattern making – did give Flossie a perfect chance to inflict self-injury. To put it lightly, he was not the most co-ordinated of people, he repeatedly dropped items and spilled his tea. Later when he bought a motorbike, he cleaned out Kings of Oxford of headlamp units for his particular make of motorcycle. He crashed or fell off his bike on average once every two weeks.

In the pattern shop - Flossie picked up a chisel he had just sharpened on the oilstone at the correct angle as per instructions given earlier by the tutor, a man who once again made the fatal mistake of leaving us to our own devices. Standing nonchalantly by his bench with the freshly sharpened tool in one hand he chucked it in the air catching it by the handle. This was not something any of us would have done and certainly not what "Flossie" should have done with his inherent lack of co-ordination but it would appear that "Flossie" had even managed to impress himself with this new-found dexterity and continued to throw the chisel ever higher into the air gaining confidence with each catch. Not only was he impressed but all of us around him were certainly impressed. Warming to this unaccustomed admiration he strolled to a bench where there were more chisels and picked up another within his reach. Now he was juggling with both hands. Soon these two chisels were joined by another as Flossie's arms whirled manically around and the chisels flashed in the reflection of the fluorescent lights, now he went into full flow with chisels spinning ever higher in the air. Such skill had not been witnessed before and Flossie slowly began to realise his predicament.

"I can't stop!" he screeched causing mass disinterest amongst all those who up until then had been encouraging him. His audience wasted away to leave him to his own fate but all were slyly watching from a safe distance waiting to see the outcome of this spectacular display. Somehow, he managed to change the rhythm so that he was tossing two in the air at a time. This allowed him, with a final flourish, to throw a pair very high in the air and then to step back so that the airborne ones descended and impaled themselves in the wood block floor.

Flossie had a brilliant mind and would leave the homework we were given at our day release at Headington Tech, until the very last moment when we got into the classroom. He would start scribbling out the answers on a handy piece of paper, so concentrated was his mind on carrying out this task that on one occasion I set light to the paper he was writing on, he didn't notice it until the flames were about three inches from his point of writing. He still handed in the remains of his work, at least he had the answer. The following week when he got in late he told Ron Pavitt, the tutor that he had lost that weeks work.

"You sure you haven't burnt it" was Ron's response.

As we were all pretty lazy at carrying out our course-work we alighted on a pretty good wheeze to minimise our efforts. We would have a discussion and disagreement on the method used and ultimately the answer to the problem posed the week before for our homework. Poor Clive Berrington, always wanting to show how good he was at solving such things, would offer his paper to convince us his application resulted in obtaining the correct answer. This was pondered over by about three of us who would hurriedly copy out his work, having agreed beforehand how much on the sheet each would copy. By way of thanks we would then alter poor Berrington's work – changing a I to either a 7 or 4 or adding a few zeros here and there to make a nonsense of his calculations, It took some time for him for the penny to drop until one week he exploded.

"Whose been altering my homework? Was it you?"

His finger pointing accusingly at one of the suspected culprits. in turn.

"Was it you?

He repeated picking out individually the likely suspects.

"Sir someone has been altering my homework".

"Oh do shut up Berrington" said the tutor Peter Hill. We knew Peter as a few years previously he had been employed as an engineer at Pressed Steel. Later when I met him he had elevated himself to the title of Professor.

"But Sir you can see this is not my writing"

Wailed Berrington to this tutor who was not the least bit interested or sympathetic.

In the mechanics laboratory Bob Anderson had dropped his pen into the well that held the water used for demonstrating certain mechanical theories. It was an expensive pen, a pen he dearly wished to retrieve. Obligingly and obeying his wishes, we lowered him into the well, upside down by holding on to his legs. Then the remaining contents of his pockets decided to discharged into the empty blackness of the water. "Bernie" Winters the tutor grimly told him he had no chance of retrieving his personal effects until the well was drained when maintenance was carried out at Christmas.

In those days press shop & toolroom floors were constructed from creosote impregnated wood blocks so that they could stand the weight of heavy castings – up to ten tons – being dropped on them. Over the years of use they were regularly anointed with further applications of machine oil and grease from the normal working practices carried out. This material was viewed, not unnaturally, by members of the workforce whenever the blocks were removed, as an ideal substitute for coal if used at home in a fireplace. Unfortunately, they took a long time to ignite but when they did boy did they go. Better than any wartime incendiary with the added bonus of thick black clouds of foul stench smoke that turned into a glutinous treacle up the chimney. The next phase was even more spectacular as this treacle then caught fire again resulting in a roaring inferno powering up the chimney and the neighbourhood being enveloped in big cloud of stinking smog by which time the fire brigade had invariably arrived on the scene and the story was set for telling the next day.

It was rather ironic that as we were being trained in the art of making wooden patterns for castings, Pressed Steel had just invented the process of using polystyrene in place of the wood. This meant that it was not necessary to employ an army of skilled patternmakers or to employ draughtsmen to design complex patterns with removable parts that would stay in the sand mould to allowing the complex overhanging parts to be extricated. These movable parts would then be removed separately. Wooden patterns weighed up to a tonne and had to be craned around the shop and into the foundry; polystyrene patterns could be carried by one man on his back, placed into a casting box, the sand packed around it and when the molten iron was poured in the polystyrene disappeared in the form of gas out of the vent holes. Wooden patterns were fine where several moulds were required from the same pattern but with "one offs", as most body tooling was, this new method was substantially cheaper and is now commonly used.

It is alleged that Pressed Steel did not make a penny out of this as they did not have a sufficiently robust patent applied for the process which was eventually used by every tooling manufacturer in the world.

The final department for our training was the drawing office - under the watchful eye of "Paddy" for Tool Design and Harry "de Train" for Body design. This allowed everyone to dispense with their overalls and into our "smart" civvy attire. The overalls were put into storage by Sid the storeman until they were required for use during our stint in the factory. Occasionally one of the tutors Brian Close, would stand in when required for the other tutors. Smartly dressed he always wore the same suit which sported razor sharp trouser creases. Everyone was convinced this suit was a good few years old but had been extremely well maintained, possibly a de mob suit as the style was so anachronistic with the lapels about six inches wide and trousers that were like vertical pipes about twelve inches diameter covering the whole of his shoes.

We were all still in the drainpipe trouser era, in fact I had gone to such extremes when I was at school that my best clothes comprised silver tight fitting drainpipe trousers and silver mock crocodile winkle picker shoes. These items I now wore with some embarrassment each time I went out but since I couldn't afford to buy any new attire they had to do. My first "drainpipes" were manufactured by my mother from a "perfectly decent pair of cavalry twill" as my father put it when he bought them for me. Working to precise instructions and measurements my Mum reduced the all-important diameter at the shoe end from twelve inches to the "de rigueur" picking out the seam from the knee and then resewing . Unfortunately, her skill was in hat making and gloves, of which several incomplete projects were stored in various cupboards around the house but she remodelled my trousers rather drastically by going from the upper larger diameter to the smaller lower diameter in a straight line. Not quite the style I had imagined, more jodhpurish than I had hoped but it did give sufficient kudos at the time until I had saved up enough money to buy the silver pair. At least my dressing style did not have any long term effect unlike Pete Broughton's. For just one day he wore to work a pair of mustard coloured trousers featuring a very large check pattern similar to that of the cartoon character "Rupert Bear". It is the name he has had to endure ever since.

Paddy had one affliction that everyone soon latched on to. He pronounced his "aitches" with a distinct emphasis on the letter "H", thus when telling us what grade pencil to use an HB [aitch bee] would come out as an "Hayyyytch bee. Ghosty [so called because his surname was Ryder] always found this affliction amusing and was totally unprepared when during one tutorial we planned mass questioning of Paddy on what pencil grades to use in certain situations. To make sure Ghosty was well warmed up we did a mimicking session of Paddy before he came to do his bit of tutoring. Off went the questions, Ghosty smirked at the first rendition of Hayyytch and with us around him whispering wait for the next one, he required judicious use of a handkerchief to cover the first signs of laughter, the next brought a requirement for a cough and noseblow. At the fourth rendition of Hayyyyyyytches Ghosty exploded into paroxysms of laughter trying desperately to smother it in his handkerchief. He wasn't helped by a phalanx of fellow apprentices indicating to him from behind Paddy's back that another Hayyyytch enquiry was on its way. Paddy by now had had enough and turfed Ghosty out of the class. Ghosty retired to the toilet to wait for us at the end of the lesson. Asked by other arrivals as to what he was doing there he recounted the episode to a fresh audience from another class and was in full flow with his impression of Paddy's aitches just as – guess who - walked in.

Harry had once been a senior engineer in the Body Design office and speculation rained as to how he had such a sudden fall from grace to be just an apprentice tutor. He was a diminutive man, barely over five foot in height and drove to work every day in an immaculate Triumph Roadster, a giant of a car. You couldn't see Harry even though he had several cushions on the driving seat which was slightly tilted by the use of wedges under the rear. Further assistance was provided by wooden blocks on each of the pedals. Harry liked to show his superiority by describing things that he thought most of us had not experienced or by using words that he thought would impress everyone. Thus when he wanted to explain why we could not be allowed to spend a day's experience in the Engineering Department because as he put it

"There's a "debago" on overtime [he meant embargo] similarly when he tried to impart his experience of flying in a passenger plane and assuming that no one else had, he stood in front of everyone declaring that wings were not rigid but flapped– Harry was now in flying mode with arms outstretched running up and down the office passageway flapping his arms to demonstrate this effect with his audience killing themselves with laughter. The alleged rumours of his fall from grace were many, as told to us lads. It was alleged that he had made some major error in the design of a car body that proved to be quite expensive to rectify.

Periodically we would be taken for a tour of the plant. Not only did we go around the press shops in R & S building we would also go to the trim shops where it was almost all female labour. The escorting guard was substantially increased as young males were preyed on. Poor innocent Ernie was ravished by a gang of them when he was sent off to the stores to get a long screw by his good friends.

Another part of the factory was the acetylene plant. The acetylene was particularly pungent but one day I went past this and walked into an Aladdin's cave. There I came across car bodies coming out of the paint shop – they were from models that had ceased volume production years ago but orders were still coming in for spare half bodies or full bodies that were put together by a handful of skilled men on the old jigs that were stored around the plant. Mostly Hillmans of 1950 vintage but the Jaguar MkII body was being made well into the early '70's with skilled lead loaders ensuring the panel joints were smooth.

At the time "T" building had originally been built as a store for pressings as the local planners, presumably having been heavily influenced by the colleges, did not want the factory to expand its production and assembly areas. Pressed Steel was a crafty organisation and no one sussed that steel framework for this new building was very substantial and had girders along its length capable of taking a crane which did in fact eventually appear with a capacity to lift ten tons. This was now the Cowley toolroom complementing the Swindon toolroom making the very large tools. There was also another area called "Small Tools" where the smaller units were made using more accurate manufacturing processes. When I was in the drawing office, one of Gordon Cattle's tales related to the time he was in an amorous situation with a young girl and thought he was impressing her with his performance when she suddenly piped up

"Are you still in Small Tools Gordon?"

At the back of the building was the pattern shop and a newly installed facility for producing prototype or low volume panels. This was the dual form press where the press tool was made from a low melting point alloy called Kirksite. The advantage of using this process was that after the pressings had been produced the Kirksite could be reheated and melted for casting the next tool.

The next building to be discovered was "U" building where a vacuum forming facility was located. This produced trim items such as facias and at that time the body for the original Ford Capri. Further along was "V" building the original "Prestcold" fridge manufacturing facility before it relocated to South Wales to be amalgamated with Jon Bloom's "Rolls Razor" facility which only lasted a few years before it went bankrupt. Rolls Royce body manufacture was located here and finished in 1980 but the most interesting area was called MPRD and comprised several small buildings at the very extreme of the plant's jurisdiction. In here were stored jigs, fixtures tool making aids and even bits of the one man submarine that Pressed Steel had made during the war. I could have spent days exploring that Aladdin's cave.

When I came into the drawing office the SY body for Rolls Royce was being tooled up for production in R Building . Little did I know that this facility would eventually become one of my responsibilities when I became a Director at Swindon but by then production had moved on to the SZ which was run by a wonderful guy called Tony Woolaston who developed a good team around him.

We all strived to obtain an ONC or HNC in order to remain as Student Apprentices but it wasn't over yet. As you went through the design office stage you were interviewed by the Chief Engineer to establish if you were suitable for entry into either the Body Design Office or The Tool Design Office. When I joined the company, I had naively thought that going into body design I would actually be designing bodies, just like I had been doing on paper as a schoolboy. Into the training programme, I found out that body design was in fact Body Engineering and appeared to me to be a pretty mundane occupation. In the days before computer graphics and 3D design a car body was styled as a clay model by the stylist, He would be responsible for the design of the exterior of the vehicle developing the proportions, shape, and surfaces. The exterior design was translated from a series of sketches or manual drawings. Progressively more detailed drawings were executed and approved. Quarter size clay "half models" were produced showing various themes and these were gradually developed until a preferred style emerged. In the centre of each "half model" a highly polished plate was inserted to reflect that half so that effectively, when viewed one side it looked like a full body style. The Body Design Department would then create full size designs, checking that all the view lines or highlights were correct. From this a full size clay model was made and then given further approval. It was covered in a plastic film to simulate a paint finish and if deemed acceptable final approval was given. Data from these models was then used to create a full-sized wooden mock-up of the final design. Bill Lyons of Jaguar would not approve his styles until they were taken out to the Pressed Steel Sports Field and viewed in natural light.

With the advent of powerful computer graphics, digitising equipment and 3/5 axis CNC milling machines, the clay model is now designed as a 3D computer model and then "carved" using the CNC machines. Even in this modern age of virtual imaging the full-size model is still the most important tool to evaluate the design of a car as it gives the onlooker a sense of security and tactile reassurance through the ability to walk around it and as a solid object.

Back to the old method – dimensions were taken from the surface of the clay and transferred onto a "layout" in the body office and then "cleaned up" to ensure a smooth shape was achieved. A wooden mock up [cube] was then made to replicate the clay and further refinement of the surface made. Dimensions were then taken off this model as if it had been sliced at regular intervals and transferred to a large aluminium sheet, painted white on one side. Onto this painted side were transferred each dimension and then scribed in with a steel point and with the aid of curves the surface of the car was developed. Once this was approved all the bracketry and minor parts were scribed onto the same painted side thus ensuring that parts did not foul each other. The body draughtsman would then lay a piece of tracing paper over the scribed component he was interested in and copy it with a pencil. He then took this to his drawing board and made a pencil copy of the component in plan and two elevations plus any details and dimensions that were required. When finished and again approved it went to the tracing department where a bunch of lovely girls copied the draughtsman's design onto a linen sheet using Indian ink. On occasions these girls, having little engineering knowledge, would copy every mark on the paper so that squashed crumbs from a lunch break or flies and other bits of detritus were religiously copied.

Once you were given one of these component drawings and the process sheet on how to turn a flat piece of metal into the component, you could design the press tools. From what I could see, this allowed you to design a series of press tools to make the components.

The assembly tool designers also had a process sheet and designed jigs and fixtures to assemble these components in a progressive series of operations from joining just two components together as an assembly to joining assemblies together as a sub assembly and these again assembled until the finished body was completed. This was much more like engineering to me!

I have gone through these processes to explain my next career move. With the rudimentary training on tool and body design, the time had come to finish our sessions at the Training School and prepare to venture out into the factory. Before that could happen a final interview and assessment of your progress was to take place with the Directors or Senior Engineers of the Body or Tool Engineering departments, basically to establish your ranking and suitability. Entering the interview room with some trepidation made even more nerve jangling by the seated hierarchy before you – there was "Jimmy James" fresh back from a stint at Yale University now Tool Engineering Director, "Rocky Hudson" Chief Body Engineer and Ozzy Osborne Body Engineering Director aided by dear old Cyril Bennett head of apprentice training. I entered the interview room and was totally ignored by the assembled hierarchy until Cyril pointed to a chair for me to sit on. They all pored over my CV. I heard a comment from Osborne.

"Hmm – he hasn't been to a Grammar School"

Down the list they went analysing your progress to date and after a few questions I was told by "Rocky" that I looked as if I might be suitable to carry on further training as a Body Engineer.

Now I dropped my bombshell

"I have decided that I don't want to go into the Body Office, I want to change and go into the Press Tool Design Office".

A sharp intake of breath followed by synchronised jaw dropping from all those seated opposite me. You could have heard a pin drop. Cyril buried his head in his hands muttering

"You can't do this"

"Rocky" glowered, Ozzy, harrumphed and left the room. "Jimmy" James was ecstatic smiling and rubbing his hands with glee

"Excellent decision" he said and as he left he said,

"Cyril sign him up to my department".

Emerging from his state of distress Cyril wailed

"Why, why, why have you done this?"

"Because it is plain to me from what I've overheard that Secondary School education is looked down on, besides I'd rather do proper design rather than copy components designed by someone else off a layout." "We'll have to look at your psychometric profile to see if we consider you suitable for your new choice"

Said Cyril and then he sank back into his quasi-religious pose, hands clasped together as if he was seeking further spiritual guidance.

An hour later I got summoned up to Jimmy James office. I thought I've really kyboshed my chances now but Jimmy was effusive.

"Well done lad you put into a few words my very thoughts, whatever comes out of old Bennet's procrastinations, you will be entering the Press Tool Design training scheme"

Highly chuffed I went back to give my mates the good news who, funnily enough, were nearly all destined for the Press Tool Design office – not that at the time that had any influence on my decision process!

Diversions

Cowley was not a particularly endearing place to spend your leisure time. In the '60's this was the period when from autumn through to winter you invariably had smog so thick that you virtually could not see more than ten feet in front of you. If it snowed, then it was not long before it turned from a pristine white to a sooty grey.

As a result of this assault on my breathing system, my sinuses became permanently blocked and after several visits to the doctor I was admitted to the ENT ward at the old John Radcliffe Hospital for a series of nasal flushings which ultimately gave little respite, So it was decided by the medics that surgery on my nasal tubes was required.

When the time came for me to have the operation to straighten things out, a local anaesthetic was applied up each nostril by the use of a small skewer covered with anaesthetic paste to numb the area of the impending operation. As I was lifted onto the trolley ready to be despatched to the operating theatre I felt two sudden twinges as the short skewers containing the paste were peremptorily removed. Into the theatre I went where I felt my head being strapped down tightly on to the table.

"Where the bloody hell are anaesthetic applicators?" This loud Australian accent boomed out followed by the Indian accent of the hospital porter who had wheeled me in.

"I took the precaution of removing them in case they got forced up his nose by accident Sir".

"You bloody idiot, I could have operated on him with bugger all anaesthetic".

The skewers were then replaced to carry out their function over the next few minutes. Blindfolded I was aware of banging and cutting around my nasal area as with the hammer, chisel and saw until the interior of my nose was modified. Wheeled back into the ward I was placed next to another chap who had obviously had a little more work done on him. As he lay there semi-comatose a sudden tirade of colourful language emanated from his mouth. I had not heard such profanities even when down in the factory. To protect my delicate ears from this barrage of swear words, I was given a sleeping potion and on waking up I thought I had gone to heaven. All I could see were flowers. Then I realised that they were on the table that went across the bed and beyond that was another bunch of flowers but no, I recognised these, they were the same as those on my mother's favourite hat and yes she was there with my Dad. They had driven up from Bournemouth to make sure I was alright. I found this a little embarrassing as I was the only male around with what looked like a florist's shop on their bed, at least the incumbent on the next bed had now stopped delivering his expletives. It was agreed that as soon as I could be discharged I could go home rather than back to the digs. Evenings in the Radcliffe were not too bad. The night time trolley came around and we were the last stop, we could finish anything that was left, as luck would have it in those days, one of recuperative tonics was Guinness so our little group would end up playing cards with the nurses drinking my favourite brew!

The day came when my previous foul-mouthed companion in the next bed was being picked up and taken home by his wife. She came in with a fresh set of clean clothes for him which he dutifully put on and finally adjusting his dog collar gave a "God Bless you all" accompanied with an ecclesiastical wave to us on the way out.

As we neared the final year of the apprenticeship, "Posy" Garland and I were given a project to carry out. It was to design and make some means to transport children around the annual sports day. We hit upon the idea of making a Dalek as in Dr. Who. This was all the rage on television. Electric tow trucks were used in factory to pull "Trains" of bogeys which carried body shells around the plant to storage areas. Our idea was to make the electric tractor unit into a Dalek and modify one of the trailers to have seating for the kids. We sketched up the designs and made mounting points to attach the Dalek body to the tractor unit. The body was made mainly of plywood from the pattern shop. The blisters or bumps that ran down the sides of the Dalek we made in the vacuum forming department situated in "V" building where they made fascias for the Ford Capri. Posy and I were ensconced in the training school pattern shop, building this object, with occasional visits by the management to see the progress, and when the Dalek was large enough Posy and I moved inside it to discuss world affairs or listen to Kenny Everett on the radio that we had smuggled in. The final touch was to do an impression of a Dalek's voice and record it onto a looped tape. Everyone was most impressed with the finished project, the only modifications required were to strengthen the mountings to avoid undue Dalek scuttle shake.

Bert, poor chap who normally drove the tractor was "volunteered" to drive this on Sports Day and was duly imprisoned as the body and bolted in. Cost implications and technical issues had made the ability to install doors for access impossible but a hinged flap was built in to allow some sort of sustenance and for Bert the driver to communicate. It was an immediate success on the day. Bert was as pleased as punch to be in constant demand towing these kids around on the trailers. Nowadays this would not have been allowed by the Health & Safety gurus [Bench seats with no backs or handrails bolted on to trailer floors] . Unfortunately for the driver it was a baking hot day but he insisted on carrying on through the afternoon. Gradually the tractor batteries began to wane and the pace of the train gradually slowed down as did the recording of the Dalek until it was barely recognisable with each vowel taking about thirty seconds to enunciate. As we had not subjected the vehicle to "Belgian Pave" road or hot climate testing some structural flaws began to show up, the most noticeable being the plastic bubbles falling off one by one and the sink plunger at the front hanging limply but this did have the benefit of providing the driver with improved ventilation. Eventually, with a few splutterings the whole thing came to a halt, to the relief of Bert and the disappointment of loads of kids, it had lasted almost to the end of the show. A perspiring Bert was released to appreciative applause from all those around and taken to the first aid tent for re-hydration.

At this time I was joined in my digs by another would be apprentice who hailed from London, he claimed his father was chief grounds man at Wimbledon. He would bring into the conversation that he had been educated at Alleyn's. Those that knew it was a public school ignored the boast and those that didn't said they had never heard of it which annoyed him greatly. He was constantly on about the brand of his clothes "My Daks trousers" or "My Austin Reed Jacket".

Pressed Steel not only pressed out panels for various car manufacturers – in fact it did work for the majority of car manufacturers making bodies for Rolls Royce, Jaguar and even made the original Ford Capri body. Its main bread and butter work was for the Rootes Group where bodies were assembled and painted and trimmed, Rootes had a particularly noticeable green paint finish, the colour of which they also used on their upmarket leather interiors. My fellow boarder somehow managed to snaffle a hide of the bright green leather and when he got it back to the digs showed it to me saying it was his intention to take it home and have it made into a leather jacket;

"Would go well with my DAKS trousers" he declared. Being a vain idiot as soon as he had it made, he wore it to work. Production of car bodies was very variable, due mostly to labour disputes in some part of the supply chain. Pressed Steel with its relatively good labour relations would carry on production and unpainted bodies destined for customers would be stored in an outside car park and sprayed with a protective wax coating. As most Rootes group bodies were delivered fully painted and trimmed to Coventry they were to all intents and purposes fully protected. Cyril Bennet, looking out of his office window was suddenly aware that of an individual swaggering like some male model through the serried ranks of painted Hillman Minx bodies wearing apparel that would have done credit to the SAS forces in terms of camouflage Here was someone who had the ability to blend in with the bodies awaiting despatch. Cyril quickly put two and two together and when I got back to the digs that night Mrs. Baker informed me that my fellow resident had been marched off her premises by the company security chief –Mr Upton [known universally as Upton O'Good] together with the offending jacket draped over the officer's arm. Upton being Chief of security modelled himself on the character Harry Lime and unsuccessfully failed to melt into the background whilst doing his surveillance or investigative duties as his trilby hat and trench coat were dead giveaways.

Travails of my Jaunts

Every weekend I would travel back to Bournemouth to see my parents and girlfriend, a herculean task to get to Poole from Cowley using British Rail. Each journey was an experience full of characters and incidents. I started catching the bus from Oxford to Reading station and then the train via Basingstoke stopping off at Eastleigh. The journey took so long that I would arrive at Parkstone station at nearly midnight and then walk the last couple of miles home to Sandbanks, but it was the cheapest way of doing the journey. One night my father came out to meet me halfway but I was so tired I did not recognise him and worst of all my pet Corgi, Bryn, came to greet me tail wagging from side to side and all I did was pat him on the head and walked past leaving a rather bemused dog sat on the pavement besides an equally nonplussed father. A few weeks later, by a stroke of good fortune, as I got off the bus at Reading station I saw a chap with rather a lot of luggage heading for my train. Offering him assistance and sitting next to him on the journey, I found out that he was a teacher and was in the process of moving house. He was going to buy a car and we arranged there and then to share transport costs and he would take me right the door – this arrangement lasted over six months. It was far better than waiting at Reading and Basingstoke and Eastleigh for the next train to arrive. It could take up to three hours to get from Reading to Poole with a winter wait in each station's waiting room huddled as close as you could get with your fellow passengers around the coke stove which was the only provision of a modicum of comfort. Everyone was breathing the heady mix of coke fumes mixed with the pungent smell of the Jeye's fluid that had been mopped around the floor in attempt to fool everyone that the cleanliness was of paramount importance. The routine amongst the regulars was then to wait for the announcement and place bets on this week's excuse that would be garbled over the tannoy system as to the cause of the delay that most trains invariably suffered. This was a major improvement in customer communication as previously you were literally left in the dark only being informed when the train came thundering in, timing the announcement of its destination perfectly so that clanking and hissing locomotive drowned out the announcers information. The Tannoy system probably being ex WWII invariably had a local announcer endowed with the broadest of accents which meant that with the accompanying cacophony of a clanking steam or diesel engine a fair bit of discussion was required with those around you to make sure you knew where you going. In winter you had a choice of excuses relayed to you for the train being late. Iced up points, fog, engine failure, signal failure were the favourite ones. In the summer it would turn to heat haze or engine failure, in autumn "leaves on line" would creep in . The regulars, placing bets, only lost when the new and creative "Cows on line" was announced.

Not believing my luck I got on the train at Reading and yes – instead of having to stand crammed up against the other passengers as was the norm – here was a vacant seat, not one but the whole bench, even better there was a table and nobody was sat opposite. Now a normal person might have found this suspicious but not me – one who seizes opportunity when it arises. I made full use of the table and unfurled my paper ready to read it. I became aware of a slight dampness around the seat of my trousers and also some of the other passengers nudging each other and giving me knowing looks. Soon I was aware that I was becoming isolated. I could not see the rest of carriage as I gradually became enveloped in a cloud of steam. It was now becoming increasingly evident that previous occupants of this seating arrangement had vacated it when the coupling for the steam heater had come adrift. Stoically I endured it for ten minutes before slowly folding up my damp limp paper I repaired casually to another part of the train where I hoped no-one would recognise me.

I first saw him at Brockenhurst station. I was on the upline carriage and he was on the downline platform dressed in very old-fashioned garb of thick tweed jacket, cap and trousers with leather gaiters. What was noticeable were his set of heavy studded boots which must have weighed a ton and which he was using with great effect in chipping up the tarmac on the edge of the platform, a pastime that he appeared to carry out with relish each time I saw him. Then one day as I was sat on my own in the compartment, I heard the clunk clunk clunk of heavy footwear coming down the corridor, the compartment door slid open and he sat opposite me. He then proceeded to start chipping up the lino on the carriage floor.

"Did a job for the vicar last week"

He suddenly mused.

"Wanted some furniture moved, Mean old bugger the vicar, offered me a cup of tea when oi'd finished"

This man was clearly of local stock, probably a frustrated Tannoy announcer.

"Oi got me own back though".

He carried on.

"As I went out down the hall I screwed me boot studs into his "parrrqay" flooring, made a fine mess it did. Not been asked to do any more work for him since".

"Very interesting"

I replied. The chipping away of the carriage floor continued.

"These boots are over twenty years old"

"Oh really",

I replied. The chipping continued then he started to swing his leg as if it were a pendulum

"Here feel that."

He said as boot swung into my shin. As the metalwork sliced into my trousers I grimaced, jumped up and told him to bugger off or I'll call the guard. Off he shuffled clunking his way down the corridor. About a year later and after several sightings of him from a safe distance, I heard the clunk clunk again, the door slid open and the carriage floor chipping began.

"Oi was down at the vicars this weekend"

I stopped him there and then

"You told me this story several months ago".

Up he got and heard a door slide open and he clunked off further down the corridor. A few minutes later there was a cry from the distant compartment. I went along to the carriage and found a slightly distressed man vigorously rubbing his shin to alleviate the sudden onslaught of pain inflicted on him.

"Did he draw blood?"

I asked,

"Yes, and he's bloody well ruined my trousers."

The journey back to Oxford was never smooth either. For some reason the timetable planners made sure that the train from Basingstoke did not connect with the Paddington train to Oxford by about three minutes, but since the London train was always late you could generally walk across the platform and catch the Oxford train just as it steamed in. Whilst waiting for the train at Christchurch it was interesting to watch the staff at work. One porter evidently had to transfer a hand cart load of boxes from one platform to another across two lines. As he lifted them off the cart he would throw the boxes across the tracks, just like a shot putt, to the opposite platform. He then noticed that the next few had a large label with FRAGILE prominently displayed on the boxes, so he picked each one of these up, walked halfway across the tracks and then shot putted them on the platform. This guy's favourite trick was to wait until you could hear the clanking of the steam train as it approached around the corner. He would then nonchalantly swagger across the tracks ready to meet those passengers disembarking so he could take their tickets. To show how accomplished he was at this finely tuned performance he gave himself the minimal amount of time to hop on to platform. He did this consistently until one day he lost his hold and white faced with a strong hint of panic slipped back on to the line scrabbling to haul himself to safety.by the narrowest of margins. Shaken and clearly distraught it was the last time this act was performed to my knowledge.

I had been told of a fellow traveller from Bournemouth who also commuted every week to Pressed Steel- Tony Atkins . He was good company and eventually when he bought a Mini we would share the costs. On one journey the train arrived at Reading and I got blocked by a slow moving passenger trying to get off with a load of luggage, Atkins had no compunction about sprinting to catch the waiting train and he clambered aboard just as it was pulling out farming out a fine flurry of ferociously animated V signs and shouting

"See Ya slow coach"

Glancing up at the now moving carriage I saw "Atlantic Coast Express" on the display board. Good old British Rail were running at least two trains late. A very tired Atkins arrived at the works the following morning, very late after having managed to hike a lift on the mail train back from Bristol. Now timekeeping was not one of Tony's attributes as he was out most nights with his drinking buddy Joe Warren and being in a bed sit, he had no one to discipline him or rouse him in the mornings. At the end of each month his boss, "Rocky" Hudson would be given the late list by the timekeepers with miscreants listed in descending order of accumulated late minutes. Tony invariably being top of the list, was summoned and told that if he didn't improve he would be sacked. The irony of this was that he would ratchet up about 120 minutes late in a month whilst the next culprit would only have about ten minutes against him. This meant that Tony, after a period of sock pulling up and alarm clock purchases, got his deficit down to below sixty minutes and was heartily congratulated by Rocky leaving the next guy on the list totally disgruntled for being ticked off for being twenty minutes late!

One thing I had to thank Tony for was for handing me his copy of Harper Lee's "To Kill a Mocking Bird". A book that had a profound effect on my attitude to colour prejudice. This was in complete contrast to my main study around this time which was William Prescott's "History of the Conquest of Mexico"

Before Atkins got his mini, an Irish chap in the body office, believe it or not he was called Paddy would give me a lift. He lived in a rented caravan at Horsepath during the week but his home was on the Isle of Wight He would fill his car up with people wishing to go via Southampton. This arrangement lasted for some time. His car was a Ford Zephyr which used a prodigious amount of petrol especially the way that Paddy drove – foot hard down swearing at anybody who dared to travel just a few miles an hour slower than his speed. One trip he got baulked for some distance by a slow moving driver and just as we got into Winchester his patience finally snapped when the driver was a few micro-seconds slow reacting to the green traffic light. Paddy leant on his horn, shouting and gesticulating through his windscreen with the usual string of Irish profanities. This now ensured that the driver was not going to react quickly, in fact he went through the whole light sequence again. Paddy by now was incandescent with rage and leaping out of his car, spurted to the offending drivers' car door, wrenched it open whilst at the same time pouring out another litany of expletives in his broad Irish accent. We watched as the diver slowly unbuckled his seat belt {the lights were now going through another sequence and were accompanied by several toots from other disgruntled drivers] as he slowly unfurled himself it was then that Paddy realised, he had possibly made a major miscalculation. This guy was well over six foot and built like the proverbial brick "S" house. Paddy turned on his heel and scampered back to the car telling us to lock all our doors. He sat in the driving seat staring ahead totally ignoring the gurning face looking through the other side of his side window. Eventually the upset motorist returned to his car to the sound of even more horns.

"That'll teach the bastard" said Paddy as he gunned the car out of Winchester. The rest of the journey was completed in utter silence.

I mention Paddy because at this time I was editor of the Apprentice Association's magazine "Paragon". Co editors were "Dan" Colin Shewry, "Moggy" Moores, Phil "Ghost" Ryder, Pete Smith did the cartoons. Now Paddy was an amateur photographer and had several photographs of models in skimpy or see through clothing which I wanted to put in the magazine. I managed to negotiate with Cyril Bennett those that he considered acceptable, but for me to get these free, I had to promise Paddy that a portrait shot of his daughter, who was not in the same league as the models, would also be published. I had a lot of flack from my fellow apprentices for wasting space on such a tame photo.

Out into the Factory

Before you could finally take up the most junior of positions in the drawing office, you had to do one final stint in the factory working on real tools and machines utilising all that you learnt in the apprentice training school. Here you learnt how the factory ran, assisted in using most of the machinery and were given simple jobs so that if you did make a mistake, the consequences would not be too disastrous. That did not apply to "Flossy's task. A hole had been wrongly punched in a bonnet and the normal remedial action was to get a slug of metal of similar size that had been pierced and weld it into the hole.This would then be smoothed off with a grinder and it would look like new. We heard a bit of commotion at the end of the shift and went to see what it was all about. A severely chastened "Flossie" was stood next a pile of bonnet panels around which a superintendent was dancing and swearing – the reason being quite obvious. Where the rogue 6mm hole had been, was a large rectangle about 100mm square laced with welding wire so that it looked just like a piece of Shreddies cereal. In attempting to weld the 6mm slug into the hole it had come from he had applied too much heat to the panel which then started to melt the area around the hole. The hole grew larger until and he hit upon the bright idea layering welding wire in a crisscross pattern over the large aperture he had created and then applying more heat tried to try to melt this into one homogenous mass. Unfortunately, this did not work on the first panel and to compound his felony – he did not get any better on the following five attempts.

I had in the meantime been put with a die fitter called "Jock". Now "Jock" had the broadest Glaswegian accent I had ever come across. Not even his fellow compatriots could understand him. I'd be stood next to a large casting and "Jock" would utter a few grunts and wave his arm in my direction. "Hoot ach och ma tottle" appeared to be the sound emanating from his mouth which combined with vigorous hand movements gave me an indication that I should get near some tools on the workbench. I tentatively touched each one in turn until I got an affirmative "aye" leaving behind the ones which got an "Och Noo" there would then follow a quick mime as to what I was to do with the selected implements. If he left the job he would leave a wee "Sweetie" and wander off confident that I was learning not only a new language, but picking up the skills to go with it.

Every day during breaktime we apprentices would climb the steel staircase to "The Bogs" which were situated one floor up, and after doing the necessary we would sit down on a large pipe running the length of one wall the toilets which carried the hot water supply. Sheer heaven in winter. There we would discuss all sorts of issues and invariably we would overrun the breaktime by several minutes. "Froggy", so called because he spoke fluent French, having married a French girl, would watch from his horizontal milling machine and as soon as he saw the slightest hint of a apprentice's green overall trying to emerge from the toilets he would pick up a hammer and start banging on his mill. It was increasingly difficult to emerge from then on as the whole of the machine shop was now on "Green" alert and the noise was deafening getting louder as one emerged. I found the best method to avoid this was to deposit a lump of metal at the base of the stairs and wait a good bit of time so that the fitters and machinists either had got fed up or thought that we all had come out. I would then slip out, pick up my bit of metal as if I had just come from having it machined and walk to my work bench, avoiding the quizzical stare of Ted Swain the foreman who loved ticking off the young 'uns. Ted had a brother who also was a foremen and wore a tweed cap that never left his head.

We basically carried out the same training regime that we had started in the training school but this time it was for real using real machines on real tools in a manufacturing environment.

At Last

My abiding memory of the first day in the drawing office was walking down the main aisle, past the Jig Design section past the planning section and Ken Adams when my eyes alighted on a rather superior looking gentleman with his feet on the table reading a newspaper. Curiosity made me ask who he was and why he was in such a relaxed frame of mind. I was told his name was Fred Law. Now Fred had been a senior manager at Beagle Aircraft, the subsidiary that the enterprising Pressed Steel Co. had bought and formed by combining the Auster and Miles aircraft companies. It had already become the largest producer of railway wagons in Europe and then, having made their money in that arena decided to sell on. Fred had been head hunted for a senior job at Pressed Steel with an office and a secretary but found on arrival that there was neither an office nor the position he had been promised and he had been dumped in the planning section at a very large table. Hence his "work to rule" until he got the got the position that he considered he had been offered. Fred would, later on in my career, take me under his wing and become my mentor, pushing me rapidly up the promotion ladder.

The next part of the drawing office induction process, was to be invited by one of the section leaders, Pete Read. to join the D.O.D.O.'s. A most illustrious club – It was an acronym for The Drawing Office Drinking Organisation and had been set up by Pete and Stan Smith who drafted the rules. The first rule being that it was incumbent on all members to promote the drinking habits of young draughtsmen. I was later to become President of the club, a post I held for some seven years. The club's headquarters was at the Crown at Toot Baldon – it is now a gastro pub called The Mole- very nice but totally different from the Crown as run by Harry Jarvey and his wife Vi. There was a short counter in the public bar and in the area laughingly called the lounge, drinks were served from a hatch that framed Harry's centre parting, Brylcreamed hair below which a mouth uttering a plethora of swear words would greet you as you entered the bar. Another fixture was "Dabber" Day a local who turned up at seven in the evening for his pint, dressed in a tweed jacket and leather gaiters, drank his fill and went back home. We youngsters used to greet him with a hearty "Yabber Dabber Do" which he used join in not knowing its origins. The pub nowadays would have had a food hygiene rating of zero as the sandwiches prepared for the Darts and Aunt Sally matches by Vi were individually stamped with a black thumbprint since these were usually made just after she had finished laying the fire, BUT her pickled onions were to die for. I still make them to her recipe.

The DODO's evolved into quite a large club. It had a small committee, so decision making was swift. "Bert" Claridge was treasurer for most of my tenure with "Ghost" Ryder the secretary. "Ghostie", was later to be my best man. Eventually he emigrated to South Africa, where Bob Admans, Pete Smith and Dave Jarrett were or were planning to be. To this day they still pop over to get the heady fix of meeting the lads. We had club ties, cravats, pullovers & even a car badge. The club logo was put out to competition for the best design and judged by Ghostie. It would feature on all club apparel. The reward for this sterling effort was a free car badge which surprisingly enough Ghostie won.

Aunty Parsons was in charge of ordering the badges and somehow managed to put the order in not once but three times which almost bankrupted the club and led to acrimonious letters from the manufacturers when we tried to blame them for over producing. Needless to say all was resolved when the paperwork emerged showing that dear old Aunty had indeed over ordered. He was called Aunty as he would do the agony column in the club magazine which exposed any club members foibles or peccadillos and certainly helped boost interest.

The President at any official DODO function at the Crown for the annual dinner had to wear the seat of office – a toilet seat rescued from Blenheim Palace by a builder friend of Pete Read's. Pete told us that the indentations on the rim of the seat

"Were the teeth marks of Winston Churchill imprinted there during an extreme bout of constipation".

This fact he would proudly explain to all those that admired this adornment.

* * *

We were given a couple of months training in the Drawing Office proper, to acquaint ourselves as to who was who and what was what. We were all as a group put under the charge of Brian AKA "Basil" Higgins. A quiet chap whose job was to impart as much of his knowledge as possible in the short time we were there before we progressed into the factory and to gain experience on how drawing office life worked. Being of a slightly retiring nature "Basil" went bright red when Harry Jarrett addressed him as" Sir", eventually managing to summon up enough courage to tell us to call him Brian in future, and that it was normal only to call those from Norman Wheeler, the office manager, upwards, "Sir". It still felt awkward for us juniors to call someone senior by their first name.

Later in my career, when I went to work in the planning department you could count on Basil to inform everyone of the impending end of the working day by is recitation of his little ditty.

"Hi de Hi de Ho only fifteen minutes to go!"

Basil's apprentice group of budding engineers was now joined by an outsider – Roger [Sambo] Sammons. Roger was a craft apprentice – not like the rest of us who were student apprentices as we had entered the company by obtaining GCE O levels. Roger had passed City & Guilds exams but had shown a very good aptitude for learning. He was also a brilliant actor and led our performances at DODO dinners. He and "Moggy" Moores belonged to the Gladiators, a club based along the Iffley Road. We would turn up as a group see their Panto each year and barrack Moggy or Sambo whenever they appeared on stage and then, as a final gesture to show our appreciation we would fire off a fusillade of several hundred paper clips at the prompt board for the inevitable audience sing along participation piece. This fusillade of paper clips was launched with the powerful assistance of a bent steel rule and were targeted at it at the end of the pointer held by Sambo. It must have been reminiscent of the English archers at Agincourt such was the quantity of metal being hurled at the board but Roger soldiered on through the sound of a thousand pings and slaps until we had exhausted our supply of ammunition.

Occasionally we would catch sight of the boss who had once been in charge of the Tool Design office –yes it was Aubrey Timberlake. "Timbers" had a retiree's problem, mainly one of having nothing to do at home which meant that he would visit the area he felt most comfortable in – his old workplace just to see that things were still running smoothly in his absence. He reminded me of Bert Lahr who played the cowardly lion in the Wizard of Oz bumbling around dispensing the knowledge accumulated in his fertile imagination to us young upstarts. He lived in a Walter Mitty world once regaling that it was he who had invented the pneumatic tyre. Coming in one day he complained that at his local flower and produce show his prize blackcurrants went missing and it was only after exhaustive investigation he found them on display in the Damson section with a certificate of commendation. He was also virtually bombproof to any sort of public humiliation. When "Jock" Sutherland had given him a verbal lashing in the middle of the office he looked totally unfazed. On this occasion after Jock had stormed off "Timbers" produced from his pockets a perfect specimen of a tomato and said,

"What do you think of this then?"

Further evidence of his horticultural expertise in his profuse production of tomatoes manifested itself each morning when he entered the office and would shout over to Norman Wheeler

"Another two pounds today Norman"

Little did he know that he was dealing with engineers and the daily declaration and tally of his harvesting achievements were duly noted so that at the end of the growing season the individual who carried out this statistical nightmare revealed to Timbers that his four greenhouse plants had produced, what must have been a world record crop of well over half a ton, a fact that when revealed to Timbers was totally accepted and ignored having absolutely no effect on his demeanour. To cap it all, when Pete Couling was relating a few stories about his amateur boxing prowess Timbers sidled up and pressing his nose to one side to indicate it was broken said "How do you think I got this then? Southern area boxing champion two years running!"

These stories from Couling are repeated every time we get together for our regular lunches and are preceded by the phrase,

"Stop me if I've told you this"

No-one has the heart to.

The PSC had an important lead in the use of Computer-Aided Design (CAD). CAD had already been established in advanced aircraft and ship design, so Pressed Steel collaborated with a Norwegian shipbuilding company from 1964 and became the first company in Europe to apply CAD to car body design and tooling manufacture. Initially this process could only do about 70% of the design element on press tools. This was done in Tony Lee's section. The part complete tool design was printed off and the missing elements put in by hand. One of the first jobs we would be given was to finish off these part completed designs. Just in front of my drawing board was an expert at this "Honky" Tom Trinder who went on to join and help develop the department which was servicing the rapidly growing Numerically Controlled facility in the toolroom. He had an Isetta three-wheel bubble car. This type of transport did not have any reverse gear and only one door which basically was the whole front end of the car. Having consumed enough alcohol to render him susceptible to an error of judgement he drove into his garage one cold winters night and stopped too close to the garage wall. After trying for an hour or so to open the car door by pushing it against the garage wall he eventually gave up when the car refused to move back and allow some means of escape. He reported in next morning having been released by his father who fortunately started work at 6.00am and had entered the garage to get his bicycle.

On the next board to him was "Nutty Slack", so called as his surname was Cole. A complete maniac in a car he delighted in racing to work and treating each roundabout on the by-pass as a chicane on a racing circuit. God help you if you were anywhere near him on a bike as you would hear the screeching tyres come ever nearer as he sent his car sideways into each roundabout in a four wheeled drift. When he got to work a lot of the time he spent constructing gliders out of drawing office materials and then launching them down the long office to see if he could beat his distance record.

Further down, Jack Butler was in charge of the die change section and had bought the old vicarage at Iffley. Jack's main preoccupation was in completing the restoration of this semi derelict but imposing property. A task that he carried out every night after leaving work taking him up to the early hours of the morning. Sleep deprivation meant that the only time he had available to top up his energy reserves, which were pretty minimal, was at work where he would dutifully sit at his desk signing off the drawings. At the other end of the office the lookouts were on duty and when the all clear had been given, "Nutty's" latest design, which had been honed to perfection, probably the mark five version was launched. It glided gracefully over the drawing boards, past the checking tables down to the Die Change area and crash landed on the comatose Jack who instinctively fell off his chair looking around to see what the hell had hit him. "Nutty" was at hand to quickly dust him down and telling Jack that he must have dozed off for a minute, the offending missile was dispatched to be stored and modified further having completely smashed not only Jack's slumbers but Nutty's distance record.

Jack had a remarkable propensity for retaining his faculties when roused from a sleep. One of the draughtsmen, Dave Wall, would delight in watching Jack writing some report and gradually slipping into the land of nod. He would then go up to Jack's desk with a pile of drawings and drop them from a considerable height. Jolted back into the real world Jack could carry on writing with scarcely a break in the smooth flow of his hand from where he had left off – pre slumber –to where he had picked up when roused.

Gordon Cattle suggested to Jack that it was ridiculously tedious having to sign off every drawing to confirm that a piece change was incorporated in the tools, moreover with so many sheets to be signed it was time consuming and tedious creeping in to Jack's slumber time.

"Wouldn't it would be a good idea to have a rubber stamp made of your signature at Hunt's in Oxford. This would allow you to increase your available rest time." suggested Gordon. Next day Jack cycled down to Oxford to order said rubber stamp. As he walked into Hunt's he started to feel around his jacket and in his pockets and with a loud "bugger" turned around and went out again. On his return the bemused sales assistant asked if there was a problem.

"I had to go back home as I suddenly realised that I had left the paper with my specimen signature behind!"

Jack was always on the lookout for a bargain in building materials and saw some marble columns on a house demolition site. He promptly cornered the site foreman and struck a deal. On his arrival at home he found the seven columns had been delivered extremely promptly, the only outstanding matter that needed resolving was how to get his daughter's car from the other side of them, a problem that took several weeks to resolve. As the building modifications progressed rewiring was required to install a circuit for a two-way switch. Jack confessed that electricity was not his strong point and got Gordon Cattle to draw up a circuit sketch with the necessary instructions. Next day in came Jack with his arm in a sling, his hand and arm badly bruised. Marching straight up to Gordon waving the instructions in his good hand he threw them down "Where does it say "Turn off the bloody power supply!"

The final section was called Metal Planning. This was where the shape of metal blanks were developed by virtually unfolding the 3D finished component into flat shape and then "lacing" it to obtain maximum utilisation from the sheet steel it was made from. Bill Allen was in charge of this area and rarely took time off for holidays.

This was a good time to be in the drawing office as the car industry was booming. The Rolls Royce Rover 2000 and Triumph 2000 [Barb] were all being tooled up at the same time, the Superminx [Audax] had just been launched and all of its derivatives were also being tooled up. One thing about the Rootes Group, they could produce a range of vehicles based on common underpinnings and by subtle changes in very few panels and brightwork they could deliver a vehicle that the customer could assume was in no way related to its cousin. This was a bit more than the badge engineering that followed where only the grille would be different. Rootes even managed to produce the Sunbeam Alpine sports car on the same production line as the Hillman Husky van/estate car shared underpinnings but obviously completely different skin panels. Around this time they could not make enough Minx's and because the replacement vehicle – the Super Minx had emerged rather larger than planned, the Minx and Superminx continued alongside each other. This was great for Pressed Steel as nearly all of Rootes products were stamped out, painted and trimmed at Cowley and the bodies transported to Coventry by Hardings Transport. It emerged that Pressed Steel was making more profit from the painted and trimmed body than Rootes were from the complete car. Unlimited overtime was available every day and at weekends to design and modify all of this tooling. To make sure that the use of skills was maximised we apprentices were allowed to work overtime on simple jobs such as modifying tool designs to incorporate any piece changes. One night only Pete Smith and I were left in the office and were having a good chat, Jack Butler had woken from his slumbers and hearing our voices decided to lean back in his chair to see if we were actually working. Not having fully woken up he miscalculated his centre of gravity and arms waving as if he was conducting an orchestra he started to fall backwards. His reactions however were quite sharp and he grabbed his umbrella, hooked the handle onto the leg of his desk and managed to arrest his fall, but this was only a temporary situation. Smithy and I continued to discretely watch how Jack was going to regain his balance. To avoid crashing backwards he was now in a bit of a predicament, as he pulled on the umbrella to achieve an upright posture, we could hear the scraping noise as the table moved towards him. Too proud to shout for assistance we watched as over the next fifteen minutes he wriggled himself into a balanced position and finally with a loud clunk he extricated himself – by which time it was time to clock off and go home.

We new apprentices generally tried to mingle in with the office rituals. Someone had brought some snuff in and we were all trying a little bit to see who could snort the most. "Nodge" was passing by. He was a large chap with a fine head of red hair and equally red big bushy sideburns –

"Resembling two squirrels running up a tree" according to Couling. Nodge now made the fatal mistake of mocking our puny efforts and the snuff provider offered him the tin. With a theatrical flourish Nodge constructed a pile the size of a bumble bee on to the back of his hand and with one loud snort hoovered the contents up one nostril. His natural red complexion went even darker, even his eyes went red; his body above his shoulders went the same shade of red. He put one arm down on the desk to balance himself as he struggled to maintain some composure, finally he slowly stumbled down the office in the direction of the toilets barking and sneezing into his handkerchief with every step. All went silent again.

"That'll teach the bugger" said Couling.

"Sass" – so called because one of the bosses had a stammer and when summoning him would call Sass...Sass Saunders, was expert at lining up copper pennies on his bent arm and catching them when he straightened it. He could do twelve no problem. Along came Nodge again to prove how many more he could do – much less, evidently, as they scattered on the floor with his first attempt. The set up was in place, now came the sting.

"Reckon you could do three or four young Potty?" Sass asked me.

"No problem, with my fast reactions it's a piece of cake" I said. "Let's make it six then".

My arm was dutifully bent to the required angle and at least eight coins placed along it. Carefully positioning me in the gangway I was advised to concentrate and do it in my own time but with a very quick action. What I hadn't taken into account was the position that they had manoeuvred me into. When. I let swing, my hand touched but a few of the coins as crucially most escaped. Off they all went into the air followed by series of loud tymphanic crashes as they splattered against a large steel pressing that had deliberately been placed against the wall. The office hierarchy leapt from their desks to see what the hell was going on – everyone else had silently and surreptitiously moved back to their boards and were studiously engaged in drafting. Some kind soul grabbed me and pushed me towards my board as Norman Wheeler and Bill Johnson came to investigate the source of this gross intrusion in office etiquette.

The Early Office Years

Des was the new boss of the office, He had taken over from Timberlake. When I first saw him he had just been promoted from the Swindon office and was very smartly dressed with a sports jacket, cavalry twill trousers, suede shoes and the proud wearer of a finely trimmed moustache. Very country gentlemanly - to complete the transformation to office manager he gradually changed his rural Oxfordshire accent to a more" college" based one. Every other manager was dressed in a dark suit or tweed sports jacket with a tie and white shirt. Des drew the line at patterned shirts and when one of draughtsmen came to work wearing a check cotton shirt he was collared by Des and told not to wear such garb in the future.

In charge of the Swindon office now was Bill Durman a soft-spoken Welshman who had, over time, honed the art of avoiding confrontation or decision making to a fine degree. When I joined the Cowley office recruiting gathered pace at Swindon. My very good friend Gary Kirk had joined the office there from Vickers [The old Supermarine factory] at roughly the same time that I entered the Cowley office. Ron Lee, a diminutive man, was the checker. He made up for his lack of height by establishing his superiority over the poor draughtsman by writing out unbelievably long snagging lists which would take you as long to correct as it did to design the tool in the first place. On joining the office Ron had bought, via a magazine, a packet of pills that claimed to stop you smoking. He was lavish in his praise as to the effectiveness of this treatment so much so that Imre Hideg, a Hungarian refugee from the uprising in the '50's, who, desperately wanting to curb his habit would try any so-called cure. Imre, who had played for his national second football team had escaped by tying himself to the underside of a train. Not wishing to miss out on the opportunity of getting one over a "bloody foreigner" Ron repacked his empty boxes with pills that his wife was having on the N.H.S.for her pregnancy. Now everyone was happy – Ron was few pounds better off and Imre was convinced he had the miracle cure.

Another member of the Swindon office was Eddie. He had the countenance of a vicar and would arrive extremely early and turn on all the lights in the office ready for the later influx of draughtsmen. After everyone had arrived the boss, Bill Durman would sneak in thinking no one had seen him and he would summon his number two in to go over the daily schedule and to basically run the office so that it did not interfere with his reading of magazines delivered from the shop floor in brown envelopes. His number two was Dave Blissett, who had been a Sergeant Major and tried to run the office in a military fashion – joking or laughing was not allowed! Each edict from Dave was referred as the latest "Ex-Blissett" instruction by the staff. Eddie, ever eager to please his boss, on hearing the outside phone ring on Dave's desk and seeing that Dave was engaged on a long discussion on the internal phone which was located on the same desk, would pick up the phone and tell the caller that unfortunately his boss is on the other phone and could he take a message.

Invariably he would then gently put the phone back on wrong cradle – cutting both callers off. Ultimately, he was moved from the vicinity of the bosses' phones, a move that caused him much despair. He was now located next to John Hemmings who was in charge of the section that modified the design of tools to incorporate engineering changes in panels. He had a phenomenal photographic memory and could recall change numbers that had been incorporated years ago on a tool reciting the ten-digit tool number, the part number the name of the part and the operations that were affected. When a few years later he was dying in hospital, he would recite these numbers randomly. Anyway, John's second career in the factory was salesmen, of such necessities as contraceptives, chocolates and anything else he thought that there might be a pent-up demand for. He was, like all with abnormal brain power, eccentric. Personal hygiene was definitely a problem. He was overweight from constant consumption of snacks, a high proportion of which was peanuts, not the ones that you could buy in any supermarket or newsagent but the ones that carried health warnings such as "Not for human consumption" they were intended for bird feeders. His lunch box had a large element of bird feathers decorating the contents as he kept budgerigars and sustenance for all in the Hemmings' household was evidently prepared on the same surfaces.

Another "New Boy" in the Swindon office was Bernard Berry – later to migrate to Cowley and to be a constant thorn in my side as he worked his way up to office manager. He arrived at Cowley with Wilf Fletcher both slotting into jobs that most of us had coveted for ourselves, they thereby acquired the title "Swindon Mafia". When he was at

Swindon, Bernard, had the misfortune to meet another new incumbent a rather short, individual called Tommy Davies who would regularly boast about the number of women he had slept with and how many at any one time.

"They probably didn't know he was there" muttered Barry Wheeler.

Well Tommy's favourite trick, which he carried out whenever he had the opportunity, was to suddenly grab the tie of one of the staff and with a magical flourish scrabble it up under their chin and producing the large office scissors pretend to cut it off. It was very convincing as you were sure he had carried out the act. Unfortunately, one time something went wrong, and he actually did shorten the tie quite considerably leaving a perplexed Berry looking over the stump of a tie protruding below his chin and then at the remains of a very nice tie curled up on his desk. Bernard was known to be more than slightly explosive and when the full reality of what had happened had sunk in he looked up, red faced, but Tommy had swiftly disappeared through the office door picking up his overcoat as he did so. The rest of the office moved to the window to watch this superb demonstration of athletic prowess as he ran out of the gates and down the road not to be seen for another day

Twice a year Des would summon the apprentices in to go over their timekeeping and attendance records. Lilian his secretary would type out the names of the apprentices in the order that they were to see Des and then usher them into the office to receive the pearls of wisdom that were to be dispensed from him. All went well until Dan Shewry, who was the next to go in decided to go the toilet en route. Des, impatient as always leapt up and barked to Lilian to send the next one in, this was Moggy Moores. This meant that Des had now managed to cock up the carefully choreographed order and Moggy went in to receive the mother and father of a bollocking for, as Des read from his sheet,

"Being consistently late AND a poor attendance record to boot!"

Lilian in the meantime, saw that Danny had come back and was waiting outside the office. She quickly informed Des of his error and with exquisite panache he picked up the correct form without batting an eyelid turned over the report and showered Moggy with compliments smoothly saying "Ah Derek, I've been watching you closely and I am most impressed with your performance. For this reason, I am going to recommend you as apprentice of the year". Moggy left smiling, as always, like a Cheshire cat, hence his nickname. Meanwhile back in the office Danny was getting an even bigger roasting, from Des. This time it was honed to perfection benefiting from the earlier rehearsal spent on Moggy.

Other trips into Des's office would be to receive your individual salary award [ISA] where the managers would get together and apportion some reward if they thought you had earned it. Paddy Flynn, who also ran the Talbot pub at Eynsham at the time, was one of the last to be called in, a sure sign that the largesse was now down to miniscule amounts. Paddy was a charming flamboyant character sporting a small handlebar moustache and long wavy hair and was always reminiscing on about his wartime experiences in Bomber Command. On emerging from Des's office he came at a fair gallop down to his desk.

"I've never been so insulted in my bloody life!" he thundered. "I put my life at risk fighting in the war for bastards like him" jabbing his finger animatedly at Des, "And he gives me an increase of half a crown, half a bloody crown. Would you believe it!!"

"Tink" Taylor looked up from his desk as Paddy's anti Des tirade carried on.

"Don't take any notice lads, the only thing he ever flew was into a rage, he was only one of the ground crew at Benson".

The ISA trip to the boss's office was a great opportunity for practical jokes, the best one was carried out in the Swindon office. Word went out that the ISA's were about to be dished out and when the managers secretary came out and asked one of the draughtsmen to go in, "Buzzer" looked up and said "They've started then. The plan was now in place – this first man called in had gone in for something unrelated to the ISA awards, just a routine enquiry from the manager but he came out with piece of paper in his hand and broad smile on his face. Going up to another draughtsman he said your next and dutifully he went in to the secretary's office had a chat with her and after a minute, he too emerged with a smile looking at his bit of paper and mouthing the word "gosh". The chain now went on, each draughtsman came out with a piece of paper and a broad smile and went to the next one. "Buzzer" was now at his wits end, the secretary couldn't understand why the whole office was coming in for a quick conversation. Eventually everyone had been in except "Buzzer" who was now animated. Asking one of the smiling recipients of the bit of paper if they were getting awards and confirmed that they were and that they were very generous ones indeed. At this point Buzzer made a bee-line for the office, burst in ranting on about missing out on awards, making a complete fool of himself to a very bemused boss who clearly thought he'd gone off his trolley.

Des had a weak point, which was that he could never remember names or recognise faces. This he would demonstrate with alarming alacrity on several occasions by stepping out of his office, pointing at a group of people and shouting out the name of someone who certainly was not within that group. This resulted in the one standing roughly in the line of trajectory of Des's finger would look over their shoulder to make sure that there wasn't anyone of that name behind them and then try to inform him of his correct identity. Des could compound this aberration still further by insisting that the new, correct name he had been given by the target of the finger point was wrong and he would confidently point out the person he thought should be identified with that moniker resulting in even further confusion for some time afterwards. He went down the office to a group of chaps and asked

"Has anyone seen Ginge Potter?". When Ginge stepped forward Des exasperatingly said

"No I want to see GINGE POTTER"

Now Ginge was so called because he had a shock of quite distinctive red hair.

"You know who Ginge is!"

Des said with a sense of exasperation in his voice increasing with his impatience at the apparent stupidity of staff who did not know their own names. He then gave perfect verbal portrait describing Mick Watts, "He sits here – got glasses and fair hair".

Mick was duly brought forward to a grateful Des who looked at the rest of us as if we were complete idiots for not recognising him immediately as Ginge. The problem now was that Mick was forever to be called Ginge by Des.

He managed to foist another name on an unsuspecting Chris Digweed who he decided had to be called "Rutledge" No one knew where it came from or who it had previously belonged to, but Des, obviously saw the name flying past in the air, grabbed it, determined that it fitted the bill for Chris [Diggers] Digweed who from then on was forever to be known as Rutledge. However, Des's main forte was getting at cross purposes when communicating. Diggers was going to Swindon every day taking drawings that required engineering changes to be incorporated. This requirement was about to come to an end and on the last trip that was to be made to Swindon, Des saw Diggers and said

"Ah Rutledge, I want you take a drawing for me to Swindon get it corrected and bring it back tomorrow"

Diggers replied

"I'm sorry Des but I won't be working there from tomorrow", assuming that Des would realise that he would return to being based in Cowley. Des was stunned and turning to his secretary said

"No one told me that Rutledge was leaving the company!" He was even more perplexed when he kept seeing him in the Cowley office.

On a similar vein he had a flash of brilliance when he was driving into work one morning and saw Mick Tuckwell waiting at the bus stop in Kidlington. Stopping, he asked Mick if he would like a lift into work which was gratefully accepted. As they approached Pressed Steel Mick said

"Thanks Des, you can drop me off here."

Des was gobsmacked when he watched Tuckers go into the shops. He was so stunned that he related the story to Phil Haines in the planning department about Tucker who had the audacity to accept a lift to work and then asked to be dropped off with no chance of getting to work on time. Phil politely told him that Tucker had actually left the office some eighteen months previous.

His best misrepresentation by far was when he discovered a sheet of paper on his desk that he had obviously put to one side to fill in later. It was a survey to be carried out in industry on the ethnic spread of engineering staff. Bear in mind that this was in the early '70s when such statistical information was not considered of high importance and political correctness certainly had not raised its ugly head. Reading the survey sheet Des found that he had only twenty-four hours to submit the results. We had one Greek chap called John Laktarides who became a good friend to me and was known to everyone as "Nick the Greek". After several years in the drawing office he returned to Greece but came to stay with us when he had to be treated for cancer in Oxford. Now Nick could not comprehend our use of nicknames for virtually everyone or how the inhabitants of particular countries got called Frogs, Krauts etc. When questioned as to what the Greeks called the English he was stumped but did come with the rather lame "Yea Yeas" which evidently was derived at that time from the Beatles song "She Loves You". He soon mastered a few Anglo Saxon swear words and taught us some Greek equivalents one of which sounded like "Skada". It was a joy to witness the look of pure petrification on his face when everyone leaving the office at night would bellow out the offending word to each other accompanied with a cheery wave. It was even worse for him when–Bill Johnson the office manager who could never pronounce John Laktarides' surname correctly and always called him Lackadorix told us he was going on holiday to Greece and sought advice on how to impress the locals. We proffered the use of this word which sounded like "Skada" and if used repeatedly would enhance his reputation. Nick was mortified when we told him what we had done, especially when Bill came back and said that using the expression meant he did not receive the best service from restaurants.

Unfortunately for Des, John Laktarides was not in the office when he had to fill in this survey form, but we did have Ken Riley. Now Ken was one of those chaps who had a very dark complexion and dark black hair. For that reason he was given the nickname "C**n Riley" instead of Ken. Desperate for information Des seized this straw and called Ken up to his office. As Ken walked in Des said

"Ah good, I need some information pronto pertaining to your family background. Sit down. Now I don't have a lot of time to fill in this form but all I need to know is where were you born?".

"Oxford" replied Ken.

"Right" said Des looking slightly quizzical

"Now listen carefully where did your parents come from?"

"Mum was from Oxford and Dad came from Liverpool".

This caused Des a little more consternation resulting much twitching of his neat moustache.

"Right I suppose that's possible, now where were your Grandparents from?"

"As far as I know Mum's came from Oxford but Dad's came from up north somewhere near Liverpool". Des was now at his wits end, time was running out for form filling.

"Look Ken, I don't want know where they bloody landed in this country I want to know which bloody country they originated from!"

"This country Des" replied Ken. Des was now driven to distraction,

"But everyone calls you "C**n" Riley so what is your ethnic background, I've got to put something down on this bloody form!"

Ken calmly explained to Des that although he had dark features he was in fact pure Anglo – Saxon and the c**n nickname was a corruption of his Christian name Ken.

"Bugger" said Des "I'll have fill this in as best I can using Nick the Greeks CV. If I was still at Swindon I'd have a whole ream of names I could use."

Ken's favourite party piece, which would always guarantee to win him a gold medal at the DODO Pub Olympics, was his ability to down a pint in under seven seconds, starting off as a warm up at just over 7.3 seconds. The games comprised shove ha'penny, skittles, Aunt Sally, darts and egg throwing. This latter event caused a problem for John Hobbs who cheated by substituting the real egg with a china one. Unfortunately, his partner's return throw was short which meant he had to dive to catch it. His main concern after his heroic catch was how he was going to explain to his wife.

"She'll never believe it was an egg" he wailed as the suspicious damp patch from the crushed object that he had secreted in his pocket spread along the front of his trousers.

One thing that gnawed away at Des's mind was that every time he looked out of his office window and saw employees clocking in they would then go and park their bikes in the sheds and then enter the office through the bottom door. This meant the loss of at least five minutes to the company each time it occurred. Deciding to take decisive action he carefully rehearsed a plan to confront these offenders and one morning stood in the office main aisle as Dave Wall entered. Pointedly raising his arm, to enhance the dramatic impression of reading his wristwatch he boomed

"You are late"

The retort from Wall put Des on the back foot. He had not expected nor rehearsed for this

"You never tell me when I'm early Des" said Mick sweeping swiftly past Des who still had his arm poised in watch reading mode and mouth wide open preparing for but unable to muster an obvious counter retort.

Around this time, they decided to introduce a cut price tea trolley service to reduce the time spent and electricity used by scores of individuals brewing up. The poor tea lady would wheel the trolley to the centre of the office with a large urn on it from at the base of which was a tap which you turned to get the delightful nectar. Dave Wall had within a few days modified a mug that had a long rubber tube coming out of its base. He would sidle up to the urn on tea lady's blind side, the rubber tube safely routed within the drawing boards where about six or seven draughtsmen were squatting waiting for the flow of tea to arrive. Turning on the tap he engaged the tea lady in playful banter, as each mug was filled a cough was given so that Mick knew when he could desist from engaging the poor lady in conversation and all mugs had been satisfactorily filled.

Soon we were to move into a new Engineering Block and Bill Johnson was in charge of the logistics. No longer were we subjected to his impression of a train as he chugged up the aisle each night in the old Engineering Block.

"Ch-Ch Ch Ch Cherio"

He would say as everyone around raised and then lowered their arms in unison to his explosive utterances as they bade him multiple farewells.

Bill must have drawn up a hundred plans of the office in an attempt to fit everyone in. It also meant that we were to have all new equipment plus the first rudimentary computer {CAD} screens. We still used drawing boards and Bill was ordering up to date equipment for the new office.

"I want to order one hundred eighteen inch metric rules"

He was heard to say over the phone and if anyone tried to interrupt him during his ordering mode he would invariably come out with

"F-F-For Christ's sake can't you see I've only got two pairs of hands!"

He would then return to marking out the footprint required for each draughtsman – table, board and cupboard. Section leaders "Radish" Radmore and Pete Read had slightly more space and the checkers – Bob Pratley, Pete Edwards and Ray Webb had a large table and shared one with whoever was next to them. Unfortunately, "Webby" and Pratley were next to each other. Webby was not a person that everyone liked, even his brother who worked at Longbridge didn't have a good word to say about him He always delighted in creating confrontation wherever he could and when Bob carefully laid out his equipment on the shared table, making sure all his stuff was in his half it only took one visit to the toilet for him to return and find that Webby had claimed an extra few inches by stacking and moving his stuff into

Bob's bailiwick. This was the stuff of border disputes and the moving of belongings from one side of the dividing line to the other continued the moment one of them left their patch. Now Bob was a bit of a gentle giant but this flagrant disregard of working space gradually escalated from the verbal reposts finally erupting into full scale fisticuffs with Gordon Cattle stepping in to try and resolve the issue which had now become known in the office as "Separate Tables", after the film of the same name. The two involved were quickly summoned up to Des's office which appeared to do the trick. All went quiet for a couple of weeks until "Radish" was caught clocking in "Webby" by one of the timekeepers This was something they had colluded between them for some time to enable them to do a bit of shopping or other activity prior to coming to work or during the lunchbreak. Up the two of them were brought into Des's office by the senior timekeeper for interrogation and disciplining for this potentially suspendable offence. As Des read out the reason for them being in front of him "Webby", who one had to admit, had pretty good acting skills, listened intently to Des outlining what had gone on, turned in exaggerated flabbergasted mode to "Radish" jabbing his finger and standing back with mock anger

"Tony what the hell did you think you were doing you should have told me."

The result of this was that it was only Radish who had to suffer a day's loss of salary.

* * *

DODO annual dinners were something special. Des would invariably stand up and give an off the cuff speech, sometimes with his glasses worn upside down or with his jacket taken off or, turning it inside out he would put it back on again' In appreciation of this heroic gesture as he finished the lads would bombard him with bread rolls. Before one of these dinners Sullivan had said he had an uncle who was constantly being mistaken for Michael Edwards, the CEO of British Leyland at that time. We made an offer to this doppelganger of a free meal and drinks if agreed to sit at the head of the table with me and Des. As we all emerged from the bar and took our places Des, being quick on the uptake, noticed that the seat next to him was empty and seizing the opportunity, grabbed the place name card to see who it was.

"Michael Edwards it can't be – not THE Michael Edwards surely!" he said repeating. "It can't be."

"It is Des" I said "He has heard so much about our organisation he insisted on coming. Can't guarantee the time that he'll arrive though." As I said that, one of the committee members at the door shouted

"He's arrived"

Ushering in a very confidant impersonator who strode imperiously to the table sitting down next to Des after shaking hands vigorously with all he passed who overacted their obsequiousness brilliantly. During this time Des had alternated between

"Christ it is him" and "No it's not, is it?"

About three or four times desperately looking at me for some sort of reassurance but we all steadfastly held our ground, ignoring Des's baleful expression for some sort of clue as if this was the real man or not. After a couple of days of letting this simmer we did let him know the true identity of the imposter and Des's reaction was one of total relief and he, guffawing, told us unconvincingly that he realised that all the time and wanted to play along with it.

Next year there was worse to come. Circular coasters for the wine glasses had been printed at work and cut out. On it read "this is a ROUND TUIT supplied courtesy of the DODO committee. Next time you hear Des say I'll get around to it, give him one of these". He had finished his meal and started to inspect his coaster. He read it and had an immediate attack of indigestion. "What bastard has done this"

He hissed through gritted teeth.

"Where did you get these printed, if these get out you could get me fired, I've always done things immediately"

Also sat next to me was Fred Law, our director,

"What if Andy Barr sees these"

I heard him ask Fred, [who was in on the joke] Fred just shrugged his shoulders and said

"No smoke without fire Des but don't worry at his level he won't know who you are."

The D.O.D.O dinners were always followed by a show, put on by fellow workmates. We even put on two musicals. The best being a parody of Oliver with Stan Simms providing the musical accompaniment on the piano. Stan, although he was a draughtsman, was also an accomplished musician. He could sight read and transcribe harmonies as if he was writing a letter. Many times he would go away for "Jam" sessions with Dudley Moore at the Goosens residence.

Back at work the following Monday Des came in early and there was instant to-ing and fro-ing between his office and Fred's. Des wanted to emphasise that he never ever let things go on without any action being taken. Later that day

I was called into Fred's office and he told me explain to Des that all the round "tuits" had been collected and destroyed as he was constantly telling Fred what he done instantly that very morning. When I told Des this he tried to make out he knew it was joke all along. Fair play to him, he never let any of this get in the way of my career prospects.

Des generally took great interest in the shows that we put on and would always ask for the scripts afterwards "So I can enjoy those jokes once more." He never got them – too much career limiting content.

Jerry Hazel worked on the next board to me and was very easy to wind up. Normally I knew when to stop but on one occasion I must have gone a bit too far. I think it was when he was telling us about his constipation and inability to strike the right balance with laxatives and binders. As he returned from the toilet I had a few jibes at him, the next thing I knew Jerry had pulled the draw out of my desk –and it was a very big drawer – and spread the contents on the floor before making a hasty exit in an extreme state of agitation once more to the toilet.

Well Jerry was a bachelor and had done service in the Royal Navy, had been about a bit and was a bit of a ladies man in his time. He now made the mistake of telling me that one of his duties in the navy had been to be a buoy jumper. This entailed dangling from the frigate he was serving on with a light rope, and climbing onto the buoy to haul in a thicker rope to moor the ship. As usual he mistimed elucidating this information, it was just before office show time and we did a song, one verse contained a reference to Gerry and "Buoy jumping" in the navy. It appeared that Des had totally absorbed all of this and when we got into work the following week, Des called Jerry up to his office. About half an hour later a red faced, very angry Hazel came stomping down to me, grabbed me by the lapels and lifting me off the floor said

"You snivelling little git you don't know what I've been through up there, you'd better get up there and tell that bastard the difference between buoy and boy." "Tell me what happened then Jerry" I asked.

"He called me in and said what an excellent show the lads had put on, I agreed with him it was very enjoyable. Then he went on to say he was very pleased with the work I had done in the office over the years, especially with introducing new young draughtsmen into office procedures AND that he had not had any adverse reports over the years regarding my predilections.

" What the hell do you mean by that?" Jerry asked

"Well you have been in charge of the new intake of youngsters over the years and I have to say not one word has come my way of any impropriety."

"What are you on about" Jerry intoned.

"Well reference was made in the show about you and bo[u]y jumping, but as I say I have every confidence in your integrity".

Before he had finished Jerry twirled round, slammed the office door and made his way very rapidly in my direction. Again, the contents of my draw found their way to the floor.

So, I went to see Des. Once again I had to go over the nuances of the script pointing out the double entendre's liberally sprinkled in it, this time I did give a copy to keep him quiet and to get Jerry off my back. Peace returned to the office for a while.

I had now applied for and got a position in the process planning department where Basil Higgins was also now working. Basil suffered from vertigo and when we moved into the new engineering block our office was on the top floor with fine views over Horspath. This was a bit too much for him so a ring of filing cabinets was placed around him to reduce the impact of seeing a horizon. One good thing emerged from this as when we were placing these cabinets around him, he told me he couldn't face climbing ladders but had just been given an extra-long one, so long it was very flexible. I bought this off him at a very good price.

* * *

These cabinets around Basil were an effective screen and all you could see were the heads of those passing by except for Roy Tuttle who was a trifle vertically challenged. Then one day all of a sudden his head appeared above the tops of the cabinets – we knew he had bought a new pair of platform heeled shoes! To make matters worse he had steel cappings on the heels so you could hear him coming and on his inaugural outing with his platforms, he got too confident and from behind the cabinets there was a almighty clatter like a thousand Gene Kellys as Tutt lost control of his footware. Everybody stopped to see what the commotion was just as Tutt's head re-emerged above the cabinets. Having gained his composure and balance he reassured us with few choice words of his wellbeing. Basil was adamant that with his vertigo he certainly would not consider wearing those shoes. He had recently been put in charge of doing the process planning for the new Rolls Royce "SZ" and he was required to visit Crewe quite often. This went fine until one day Ellis

Shaw came in from the body office and told him he was going up to Crewe so he would take Basil with him. The journey up did not go well for Basil, who on arrival at Crewe, had to have a lengthy rest to compose himself after the excesses of Ellis's erratic driving. Ellis must have had about size 14 feet and was not the most co-ordinated of people. On setting off for a trip his plates of meat would descend on the accelerator pedal forcing it firmly to the floor. Having regained some of his composure, Basil summoned up enough courage before they did the return trip to broach the subject of Ellis's driving style confessing that he suffered from travel sickness and that he would really appreciate it if Ellis could keep under forty miles an hour. Ellis was profuse in his apologies and told Basil that he really should have piped up earlier. So off they set. All was going well until they came up behind a large vehicle going slightly slower than desired speed limit and so the overtaking manoeuvre was initiated. Soon a lorry appeared on the horizon travelling towards them but now occupying the same side of the road. Ellis pressed on gamely – at forty miles an hour -the distant lorry was now getting much closer. Basil lost his cool and shouted at Ellis

"Put your bloody foot down!"

Which he duly did just avoiding the horn blaring brightly lit flashing wall of steel by the skin of his teeth.

Basil never travelled with Ellis again.

* * *

Brian Sullivan used to delight in creating trouble for Des by the simple expedient of picking up one of Des's directives, periodically issued to staff to reinforce his position and authority. Analysing each missive to see if the contents had not been fully thought through or might have unintended consequences. Brian would then get the secretary to type out a memo highlighting the repercussions if Des's memo should it be put into action. Careful timing was now required to make sure that Des had his copy and that Jimmy James was away from the plant. With a quiet "Watch this" from Sullivan, as his timebomb was activated we all watched the ensuing panic and rapid movements from office to office as Des tried to intercept the copy that was to go to Jimmy. Sully would have immense pleasure watching this.

For Des to obtain membership of the Institute of Mechanical Engineers he and Jimmy James [tooling director] had to give a presentation in Oxford Town Hall on the intricacies of tool design and metal forming. Des tasked me with drafting out the presentation and overhead slides and as I went over it with him it became apparent that he had difficulty in getting his tongue around the word technological. As the presentation was honed to perfection and the great day approached, Des was called away to another factory and asked me to go through the final draft to make sure there were no errors. This gave me the opportunity to sprinkle a few "Technologicals" into the presentation before his secretary typed it up. Come the great day, in front of the great and good Des stood up to give his part of the dialogue to the overhead presentation, all going well until the first "T" word appeared. After three utterances of "Technololol" he managed to substitute the word " Complex" for it then on the next one after some more attempts the word "difficult" was substituted. He managed to sidestep the next two by some quick thinking and finished his session mopping his brow with obvious relief. I left the proceedings quickly as I was sure I would be confronted over the issue. Next day to be sure, he marched into his office, I heard the door slam and within a minute I was summonsed in to see him. I quickly congratulated him on excellent performance. He said

"You didn't notice any obvious fluffs then, but where the hell did all those technological's creep into the script."

"Well" I said, "They were always there, perhaps you didn't notice them, I didn't notice any problems with your delivery which I thought was excellent."

He let me do a few more scripts for him after that. To this day all of us who worked for him regard Des with great affection. All in all he was a good Boss. To ensure his memory would be long abiding – he made sure that no printed document went out of his department without his moniker on it. Some of these must still exist at Cowley and other parts of the car industry.

* * *

Around the same time, Fred Law had taken over tool engineering as a director after Jimmy James had died of cancer. I think that by now I was clearly on Des's radar and I was one of the few people he could instantly recognise and put a name to with confidence. "Dave, will you report to Ken Bradbury's office there's a project to be done."

Ken was the top Director for all plants that designed, made or ran press tools in the now British Leyland empire. He had started from very humble beginnings and knew Des from his Swindon days. Ken's family were basically on the breadline and he would come into work in those days in threadbare clothes and shoes that were falling apart. He was one of those characters who was determined to better himself and did so, becoming a director in several companies. British Leyland, as it was now known, employed over 250,000 people and had well over forty manufacturing plants spread across the country. Certainly, a degree of rationalisation was called for. In the toolmaking and pressing plants, there were Castle Bromwich, Drews Lane, Longbridge, Solihull, Browns Lane, Canley, Swindon, Cowley, Speke, Llanelli, Dunstable plus Linwood in Scotland to name but a few.

I duly reported to Ken who outlined what we had to do. It was to draw up a matrix of all the plants under his control and then detail the number of people employed in what capacity and, if similar activities were being carried out elsewhere, how reliable they had been in service. This was all hush hush as we "red ringed" those who had not achieved the criteria and started to see who would be most likely to accept transfer to other plants. I got so engrossed in this that I was missing out on my several cups of strong coffee and started to have the "tremors" or shaking hands. Initially I thought it was stress but soon realised it was caffeine withdrawal symptoms. I really liked my coffee *very very* strong. After a few weeks I had drawn up a scenario for rationalisation and went over it with Ken. He made a few modifications and then told me take the plan to H.Q. I went to book a car to go and found that there were none available, so I went back into Ken's office and told him I couldn't get a car,

"What's wrong with yours he asked?"

"I'm not insured for company business" I replied. "You don't have a company car. What bloody grade are you? When I told him I was not management grade he almost collapsed.

"Right lad you are clearly in the wrong grade, I'll correct that straight away – you do realise that what you have been working on does not go outside these four walls!"

Within a day I had my new grade, signed the company's "secrets act" and had a new company car From my point of view it was the best thing that Des had done.

Several months later Des sadly, passed away in Japan whilst carrying out company business.

He was sadly missed by all of those who worked for him. He was a great character.

The Class of '61

Bob Danny, Bin, Rupert, Moggy, Ghosty, Hairy, 'Arry, Harry, Sambo, Smiffy.

These were our nicknames of the '61 intake of apprentices into the drawing office the only infiltrator being Sambo, who was a craft apprentice and somehow managed to inveigle his way into student apprentice territory. He ultimately managed to do better than any of us by obtaining a Master's Degree, due as we all maintained, to the fact that he had so much spare time he could do a lot of swotting.

As each of our twenty first birthdays came up we chipped in to have these nicknames engraved on a pewter pint mug and we would embark on a tour of the Oxford High Street pubs. A pint in each one was the aim. There was one small flaw in this process – I couldn't consume more than two pints before I became embarrassingly ill. My favourite tipple at that time was bottled Guinness which did help to ameliorate the problem as it came in half pint bottles and as it was a slightly stronger brew than the then current beers it did present a slight face saving get out. Nevertheless I was still known as "Two Guinness Chambers" and whilst I was an active participant at the first pubs on our sorties I was invariably carried into the last pubs on the shoulders of my not very sympathetic compatriots who chanted the mantra coined by Moggy Moores "Cream buns and fatty bacon!"

This was designed to assist in ones rapid recovery and general feeling of well being. I did manage to recognise the final pubs – The Wheatsheaf, Chequers, Whites Bar and finally The Old Tom by the decoration on the ceilings as this was all I could see when I was transported into each bar and laid to rest on a suitable bench as the rest caroused noisily. Our picking up point was, believe it or not, the steps of the police station where we would wait for Bob Admans to bring his old Hillman Minx lurching down St Aldates towards us. Invariably, and this says a lot on how relations between the police and the public have changed, we would engage in conversation with a constable who would make sure we were loaded into the car in a seemly fashion and with a stern warning to Bob not to drive faster than twenty miles an hour he would then see us on our way.

* * *

On another night as we did the rounds of the Oxford pubs one of our group "Dan" Shewry, let on that his old man did the window cleaning for Woolworths. This was too good an opportunity to miss and Dan's father was duly called later that night by the *"Woolworth's Store Manager* and told in no uncertain terms that having just walked along Cornmarket he had looked at the store and was horrified at the slipshod workmanship employed to clean the glass. Within the hour, as we sat in the Golden Cross bar enjoying a pint we amused ourselves watching Dan's father going over all the large windows with the utmost care making sure all the little bits in the corners were clean and smear free.

* * *

Dan almost drowned a few months later, not through swimming not even in water. One night when we finished one of these drinking treks we went to the Golden Palace Chinese restaurant. By this time having only drunk two Guinness, I had recovered but Dan was definitely the worse for wear in spite of having visited the toilet several times. He came back to the table sat down with that far away fixed expression that inebriates adopt, and then quietly fell asleep with his head in a large bowl of chicken noodle soup. Luckily an attentive waiter saw him blowing bubbles in the broth, managed to grab his hair and fish him out thus preventing him from drowning. Everyone else carried on as if this was a regular event which to certain extent it was because "things" happened in Chinese restaurants. In those days, another favourite stopping off point was the Kum Ling in the Cowley Road where you had to pass through the kitchens to get to the toilet. Full of good humour we finished off the evening by leaving the money for the bill with a slight sprinkling of Soy Sauce on the notes and departed. The waiter must have thought that we were doing a runner for as we sauntered off down the road, a chef brandishing a machete suddenly appeared from an alleyway screaming at the top of his voice, behind us two breathless waiters ran up claiming that we had not paid the bill. A short trip back to the table to show them where the money was, resulting in profound apologies all round and a few more drops of Soy Sauce for good measure on our part.

During one of these soirees it was decided that, for a change, we would visit the Turf Tavern. A quaint pub that could only be reached by a couple of narrow alleyways. Bin led the way and halfway down the alleyway he collided with a roadsign prominently displaying the word "Roadworks".

"Bloody students" muttered Bin as he pushed us all back using the sign as a cattle prod. Having cleared the obstruction Bin led us back down the alley. I was right behind him with the rest of the lads behind me, I looked back to see if everyone was in tow and someone said.

"Where's Bin?".

I turned again to go forward – No Bin! From the gloom of the alley I was conscious of a flurry of hands and legs and a scrambling sound by my feet, looking down I could see this white face peering up from the bottom of a six foot deep hole. He was desperately trying to maintain some dignity by clawing his way back to the top – not a sound had he uttered until he was back on terra firma. "Bloody students" he repeated. On another occasion we lost "Arry" Goddard, couldn't find him anywhere. We were not unduly concerned and decided to drive home. A good way along the Abingdon

Road we came across "Arry" stumbling his way home like an obedient dog heading for its kennel. We picked him up and propped him up outside his mother's house and then carried on in Phil's Morris Minor dropping off other members of our group on the way.

The furthest out was Rupert who lived in Long Hanborough. Halfway there we would always say we had an urgent requirement to relieve ourselves and Phil would obligingly pull into the same layby each time. Someone had noticed that there was a large stack of used bricks by the hedge we used for relieving ourselves and consequently each of us would dutifully pick one up and take it back to the car. Phil would then come to work the following morning complaining about the additional cargo he had acquired. Soon the complaints stopped but we still carried out the task – about four to six bricks each trip in the rear footwell. Later we found that reason for the reduction in complaints was because Phil's father decided he had enough bricks to lay a small wall in the garden.

Phil's car did valiant service on the twenty-first birthday trips. The furthest celebration was out in Banbury where Harry Goddard had an uncle who was landlord of a pub. The trip there was interesting to start with. With four of us in an old side valve powered Minor it was bit sluggish. Phil got behind a transporter carrying car bodies to the Midlands. As he was running out of straight road to complete a rather cumbersome overtaking manoeuvre he decided to cut in and get between the lorry he was overtaking and the one in front of it. He soon realised that it was not a lorry he was overtaking but a trailer being towed by a lorry of similar size. His sense of panic was evident in his language both bodily and verbal as he tucked in between the lorry and trailer with a few inches to spare at the front of the Morris and the rear. What really concentrated his mind was that he had a similar amount of distance from the side of the car to the trailer's tow-bar and could not get fully tucked into to avoid the oncoming traffic. He watched, white faced as the oncoming traffic came towards him, some flashing, finally he got to another stretch of road where he gingerly moved the car from its mobile entrapment and again completed the long sluggish move past the lorry up to the next layby where he pulled in, mentally exhausted at his brush with death. Naturally, we all thought it was huge joke. We all went for a Chinese meal returning to the pub where 'Arry's uncle had thoughtfully provided a barrel of beer and ultimately went to sleep. I remember waking up and seeing 'Arry with his head under the slow dripping beer tap his eye socket acting as a receptacle. The next week as a form of recuperation we all went the Nottingham Goose Fair. Unfortunately, Ghostie had got the dates wrong. We were a week late.

Pressed Steel was flush with money and was, perhaps the world leader at this time in using computers to design press tools. The system was IBM based and the method employed at the start was to part design simple tools. Computers at this time were not powerful enough to design a complete tool but could carry out the basics. This information was put onto punch cards by a designer and then taken over to the computer room in the Fire station Block, put through a reader and the basic design would be plotted using a flatbed Gerber printer. This 80% design would then be brought back to the design office for the designer to complete the more complex parts of the tool. Bill Emerson was in charge of

CAD development in the Research & Development block and the company made one dramatic blunder that saw him leave the firm. They put a full-page advert in the national papers with Bill's photo and his full CV under it describing what he had achieved and his plans for the future of CAD development. Needless to say the job offers streamed in.

* * *

All was going swimmingly in Tooling. We had the largest toolroom in Europe and press shop in Swindon. We were designing and making tools for many Continental car plants, I can remember going down to "C" building where they were crating up tools for dispatch to Alfa Romeo, one tool was late in tryout and had be boxed up and sent to the docks with fitters still inside completing the work. Having decided that I wanted to move from Tool Design, I applied for a vacancy in the estimating department. I got the job without even completing the interview. Ossy Davies, the head of department, was clearly by his accent, a Welshman and reading my application form excitedly said

"Your Welsh, born in Swansea! Looks like you've got all the correct experience and qualifications you can start as soon as you like."

Now Ken Webb, his deputy decided to take a more cautious approach and telling Ossie firmly that nationality was not the sole criteria for getting the job and started to probe my experience by asking some difficult technical questions. Whilst in the background Ossie was still saying

"As far as I'm concerned the position is his". With the interview finished I was told I should have some news in two days.

Going back to my drawing board I was surprised to learn that another interview I had attended some weeks previously was successful and I could start in the planning department A.S.A.P. which I was only too happy to accept.

The first project in this department was a complete new body for Hyundai's first car – the Pony. A few Korean guys had come over to learn from the process and each day they would unscrew some tin canisters and the foulest stench you can imagine emanated from these containers. Evidently the contents were a form of cabbage that had been buried for months and had fermented and rotted in the tins and was to our surprise highly regarded as a delicacy by our Korean friends.

Workmates

Bin

He and "Arry" Goddard have been my friends for the longest time. Bin has survived my taunts and practical jokes for over fifty years and we still go on holiday together with our respective long suffering partners. Bin wasn't in my group of apprentices in the first part of our training but according to him he had anecdotal knowledge of my exploits. It was when we were doing drawing office training that we collided and there was John with a natty hat which had a little feather stuck in the band above the rim. He had a car and would offer me a lift occasionally. To repay this courtesy I got an empty packet of contraceptives from the office purveyor and stuck it in the hat band over that little feather. Off he marched unknowingly displaying the well-known brand of rubber goods, beaming at those who were smiling at this pretty good impression of the popular cartoon of the Mad Hatter at Alice's tea party. His girlfriend, Pat was not amused and suggested that as I was such a little squirt he should punch me one because he was going home and complaining each day that this little runt Chambers was winding him up. He really played into my hands – I used call him Edmundo Ross as frequently I would hear a clunk, followed by a "Bugger" and there he would be shaking his Thermos flask like a maraca players doing a very good impression of the Latin American rhythm player considering its contents comprised broken glass and tea. We eventually bought a kettle so that problem was solved but as he made his first foray into the world of instant coffee new problems conspired to work against him. Having used three quarters of the contents of one jar he went out and bought another of similar size. Forgetting one of the basic elements of his education in which words Archimedes and Principle were of paramount importance he, for some inexplicable reason, tipped the contents of the full jar into the partly empty jar. Another "Bugger" meant that his shoes and a fair bit of the office floor were the recipients of a considerable dusting of coffee powder. Granules would have been easier to clear up but they were a new product and much more expensive and the cleaner was moaning for days after as she tried to remove the sticky compound from the floor.

Another coffee instance happened when I was promoted to the planning department. One of my workmates, Roy Tuttle, would regularly come down and ask if he could have some coffee as he had run out. This happened so often that I decided to put an end to it with a carefully constructed ploy. I bought some gravy powder, filled the coffee jar up with it and placed it in the usual position in my draw. I then hid the genuine article in another draw. For some reason it took Tuttle some time to run out again but eventually he came down.

"Can I have spoonful of coffee Dave?"

He asked.

"Sure"

I said as he scooped a generous portion into his mug. Walking back to his desk I watched him sniff the contents.

"Christ this must be some cheap stuff you've got here, it smells just like gravy!"

The rest of my workmates who were clued up on the proceedings watched as he poured hot water into the mug and vigorously stirred it. "Doesn't dissolve as easily as proper coffee" was his next remark. The mug now stood by his right hand for ages as we all expectantly waited for the first sip.

"Tell you what Dave"

Tuttle looked as if he had a bright idea.

"Why don't you actually put gravy powder in a jar and offer it to the lads. God, I'd like to watch their reaction, If anyone did that to me I'd plant one on them!".

He took a large swig out of his mug followed by an immediate regurgitation of the obvious foul-tasting liquid coupled with a gurgling "Bastard!" This trick had unintended consequences when Couling came and told me that some engineers from Jaguar were down and as he did not have much coffee he had used mine. We just managed to rescue the situation in time before any contact twixt cup and lips had been made.

Bin and I started to go out lunch times for a bit of relaxation to one of the pubs near the works. The Chequers at Horspath was ideally close and a gang of us went in and ordered a few pints. As we were sat down a group of girls came in and Lothario Bin, ever the gentleman, stood up to allow them to get to their table. The first hint that something was about to go wrong was when a loud crash came from behind him as about twenty knives fell off the table that he had tilted when he moved his chair back. At the same time he was halfway through carrying out a most courteous and majestic sweep of his arm in true Shakespearian style embellished by a phoney French utterance of "Madame"

CRASH – the arm went back to his side as the sound of another set of knives hitting the stone flagged floor followed by the sound of smashing glass as the pint pot that had contained them also hit the floor – CRASH – now it was the turn of spoons to follow the same cycle. It wasn't over yet but he thought it was. Another three or four crashes came out in rapid succession as the back-up pint mugs stored further back also took their turn to ratchet up his embarrassment.

"Thank god serviettes are made of paper"

Someone said as poor Bin attemted to clean up the mess he had created.

Another glass related story occurred because when the working week was reduced the simplest expedient for the Company was to knock the time off at the end of the week so that we finished at midday. It was a glorious sunny summer afternoon; a group of chaps were enjoying a game of Aunt Sally and we were sat at a picnic table in the garden of the Three Horseshoes enjoying the ambience. As the glasses emptied my good friend suddenly moved to scoop up the empty glasses, "let's have another!" and slid along the seat of the table. In his haste for another drink he had forgotten that the bench seat was actually attached to the table at either end and the next thing I saw was him upside down with his nose in the grass and his legs kicking in the air . Self preservation had obviously come to the fore and realising that holding two pint glasses whilst you were plummeting earthwards could result in serious injury he managed to jettison them by hurling them as far away as possible. The first glass landed and smashed in front of one of the Aunt Sally players just as he was about to throw his stick, as they looked around to see where it came from the second landed within their group.

Looking for culprits all they could see was me with an air of innocence trying to stifle a laugh and some idiot kicking his legs in the air writhing half on and half off one of the picnic tables. Bin did have the good grace to apologise and clear up the glass shrapnel.

He was also adept at quirky turns of phrase which became embedded in every day conversations, phrases such as "Uttering gutturals" when referring to the use of coarse language or "Folds of whatever". When describing an ample female form.

Place names were truncated. Kingston Bagpuize would be modified to "King Bag"

Still we put up with his funny ways.

"Arry"

It was around this time that I managed to catch out one of my best mates "Arry" Goddard, with what Pete Couling called a superlative prank. Poor Harry had a morbid fear of donating blood and kept putting it off. In those days most of us donated blood regularly. He eventually summoned up the courage to attend the blood transfusion unit that set up camp with a few beds in the Gym in the training school As I came to go back to the office after giving my pint I stumbled across an ashen faced Goddard sat on one of the steps.

"Are you alright?" I asked

"No I feel a little faint" was the reply.

"You'll feel better in a couple of hours, let me know if you have any other concerns and I'll tell if they are normal or not."

Over the next twenty-four hours he checked out twinges and pain with me.

"Look it's gone all black where they stuck the needle in. I'm also getting sharp pains across my shoulders and down my arms. Did you have these?"

This was what I'd been waiting for. I rang him on the office phone putting on my best Scottish accent.

"This is Doctor Muir here. I understand you've recently donated some blood".

"Yes, Yes I have" said an evidently relieved Goddard that at last he had someone with a modicum of medical experience to share his concerns.

"Well I've just had the lab test report from the Churchill on your blood sample. Now, have you got any pain or discomfort where the needle went in?

"Yes yes" he interjected "and I've *----"

"Just let me do the asking please" I carried on with my soft Scottish accent

"It's gone all blue!" blurted 'Arry".

"Right", I said, "Any pains across the shoulders?"

"Yes Yes Yes" He blurted

"Is this normal?"

"No it isn't but it is entirely symptomatic of the analysis report that I have here. Now I don't want to alarm but could you RUSH over to the works hospital here now!"

"Arry" did indeed rush over, running down the corridor to the reception. "Dr. Muir, Dr Muir he wants to see me".

"I don't think so"

Said the receptionist

"He's gone to Glasgow. You are not the first one to report here today, you know what day it is"

She said pointing to April 1st on the calendar.

"Bloody Chambers"

Was all Goddard could come out with as he found his way to Moggy Moore's office. He'd stayed there for some time hoping to cause me some concern over his prolonged absence.

Dick

Dick Baigent had a favourite trick. When the coast was clear he would run up to the layout tables – these were about twelve feet long – lift his legs in the air just as he approached the end of the table and slide the length on his backside dropping off gently at the far end as the momentum decreased. He could be very easily egged on to carry out this quite impressive act and sure enough he would nearly always oblige our

"Go on Dick give it a go".

The timing now was critical. One of us psyched Dick up to give it his best and as we cleared & polished the table and holding him back from launching himself until a signal was given by a lookout stationed at the window. At the right moment Dick launched himself only this time a handful of drawing pins had been carefully chucked on to the table resulting in a banshee like cry resonating around the office just as Des walked in.

Ken

It happened quite by accident. Ken Bull, always a natty dresser came in one day wearing a thick plastic raincoat – not the cheap showerproof type – but a designer plastic raincoat. From then on whenever he wore it "Here comes the PVC coated K Bull" would ring out. Pete Couling was quick to latch on the endless possibilities of this so it didn't take long for Ken to be called over, offered a red ball point pen, then asked to put his signature on a piece of paper and after Ken had duly complied

"Inkredabull"

A triumphant Couling declared, "Have you wondered why Des singled you out for promotion?"

"No," said Ken

Despickabull"

And so it went on, day after day until the joke wore so thin and Ken would refuse to come and see us which was a bit of a problem as sometimes there was a genuine reason for wanting to see him and discuss something.

The Afterglow

Even after we had all retired we would meet up now and again and then we would all come armed with "Bullisms". Ken had tried to counter our attack by going on the web to see if he could come up with some reposts but gave up when he saw that there were over 800 possibilities of "Bullisms" especially when photographs started to be taken at the pub of him entering [Bull at the gate]. In the doorway [Adorable]

Pete Taylor started to feel the heat when these gatherings which were held at the Oxford Yeoman at Freeland, a particularly confusing place for the first time visitor as it had three gates in the fence and three doors to the bar. On Taylors' first outing we all watched from the comfort of the bar as Pete first tried to get into the pub through the wrong gate returning to the road to suss out why had chosen the wrong one. He then then he had to choose a door. Starting on the left door he went into the toilets, he then came out tried the next one into the kitchens and then finally arriving in the bar to loud cheers from a grinning crowd giving him the thumbs up.

Regular get togethers are still held. There is what is called the Bob Taylor's mob comprising mostly estimators and organised by Kevin McAllugh or Muckerlug as Couling calls him, plus a few toolroom stalwarts. Then there is the die office group of Kirky, Maurice Smith, "Arry" Goddard and Barry Wheeler although a "Jigolo" as Kirky calls him, as he hails from the Jig Design office, Brian Reason now comes. We also have a grand Xmas bash organised by Arry with about 40 attendees. As time passes on so do we.

* * *

I was now on a career path that would ultimately see me as a director and it is not half as interesting and fun filled as my early working life which I have described up to this point, although I have could have put in this resume' at least as much again. I have worked with some wonderful people, enjoyed their company and friendship. As all "Old Timers" say, "It's not the same now as it used to be."

I think the introduction of the computer workstation signalled the end of friendly banter and had a major effect on office camaraderie.

C'est la vie.

Buses & Bikes

App 1

Information supplied courtesy of Brian Reason from an old archived document retreived from a wastebin.

COMPANY	ACTIVITY IN PRESSED STEEL
Foden	Cab pressing & Assembly
Hillman	Pressings & Assembly
Ford	Pressings & Assembly
Accles & Pollock	Garden tables
Humber	Assemblies for light car
BSA	Body based on Minx salloon
AJS	Mods to Minx Saloon to fit on chassis
Pyrene	Stampings
Karrier	3 wheeled tractor,Stampings
Morris Commercial	Cab production & Assemblies
Marco Refrigeration	Cabinets
General Motors	Chassis frames
Daimler	Chassis parts
Wolseley	Engine sump, body pressings
Austin	Body panels

Vauxhall	Body parts
Wood Alex	Animal feeding trough
Cambridge Instruments	Indicator case
Guy Motors	Dash
Chadson Radiator	Radiator parts
Brush Electrical	Steel boxes
Armstrong Siddeley	Brake drums
Tecalemit	Drum covers for brakes
Rover	Body panels
BTH	Refrigerator parts
Lanchester	Parts for 10HP Saloon
Mann Egerton	Seat brackets
Orme Evans	
[Wolverhampton]	Pressed steel baths
Chevrolet	Chassis parts
Theatre seats	Quotation

Celebrations

A farewell send off before they set off for pastures new in South Africa

Phil Ryder, Dave Chambers, Pete Smith, Paul Goddard, ?,
Dave Jarrett, Moggy Moores and Bob Admans

DODO Dinners

Fred Law, Dave Chambers and Des Allsopp

Dave Chambers with the Seat of Office Des Allsopp

Fred Law, Dave Chambers, Des Allsopp and Brian Cobb

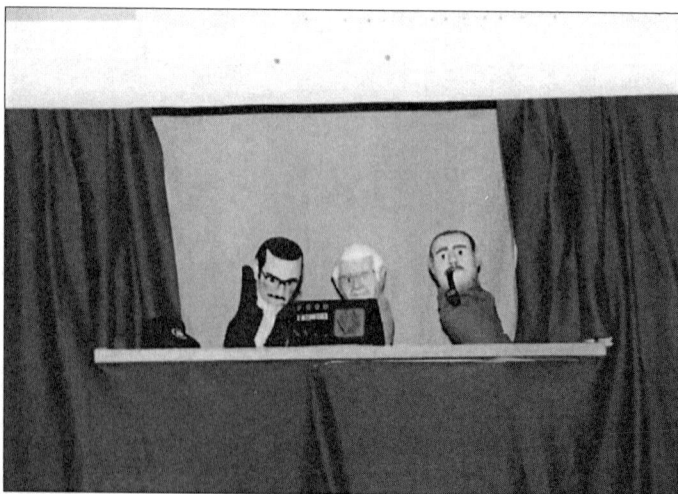

A Typical Office Sketch with puppets featuring Des Allsopp, Dave Blisset and Tubby Leach

Acknowledgements

To all who have contributed to the events recorded. I wish I had written everything down at the time and not have to rely on my memory.

Bonnie, for waiting patiently for me to come down from typing in my office to take her for a walk .

Carol, my wife, for helping me with the book.